101
Winning Racing Strategies for Runners

Jason R. Karp, Ph.D.

©2012 Coaches Choice. All rights reserved. Printed in the United States.

No part of this book may be reproduced, stored in a retrieval system, or transmitted, in any form or by any means, electronic, mechanical, photocopying, recording, or otherwise, without the prior permission of Coaches Choice. Throughout this book, the masculine shall be deemed to include the feminine and vice versa.

ISBN: 978-1-60679-198-1
Library of Congress Control Number: 2012930353
Cover design: Studio J Art & Design
Book layout: Studio J Art & Design
Front cover photo: Courtesy of Jason Karp

Coaches Choice
P.O. Box 1828
Monterey, CA 93942
www.coacheschoice.com

Dedication

To my mother, Muriel, who never stopped telling me how proud she was of me, who attended all of my races, and who taught me how to lead a winning life.

Acknowledgments

Thanks to James Peterson, Angie Perry, Kristi Huelsing, and the rest of the editorial staff at Coaches Choice; my wonderful agent, Grace Freedson; my twin brother, Jack, for inspiring me to be as good of a writer as him; Hadar Elbaz, for adding beauty and grace to the book's cover; and the many runners I have coached, from whose races I have learned a great deal.

Contents

Dedication 3
Acknowledgments 4
Introduction 9
Chapter 1: Winning Training for Racing Strategies 11
#1: Train smarter.
#2: Train with a good coach.
#3: Have a training plan.
#4: Run more.
#5: Improve running mechanics.
#6: Improve aerobic base.
#7: Improve acidosis threshold speed.
#8: Spend time running at faster speeds.
#9: Increase $\dot{V}O_2$max.
#10: Increase anaerobic capacity.
#11: Maximize recovery.
#12: Get more powerful muscles.
#13: Train with others.
#14: Understand adaptation, and train progressively.
#15: Taper training before important races.
#16: Become very familiar with what different paces feel like.
#17: Periodize training.
#18: Practice running hills.
#19: Run time trials.
#20: Develop a finishing kick.
#21: Use interval training wisely.
#22: When training for a marathon, don't consume carbohydrates during long training runs.
#23: Train to strengths.
#24: Get a bigger heart.
#25: Live at altitude, but train at sea level.

#26: Train consistently.
#27: Train with a purpose.
#28: Use benchmarks.

Chapter 2: Winning Pre-Racing Strategies 45

#29: Know the opponent's strengths and weaknesses, and capitalize on them.
#30: Hydrate.
#31: Play head games with opponents.
#32: Visualize the race before it happens.
#33: Know what pace can be sustained in the race.
#34: Consume caffeine before the race.
#35: Give a self-pep talk before the race.
#36: Have specific, meaningful goals in mind for the race.
#37: Have a race plan.
#38: Go to the bathroom before the race.
#39: Get to the race with plenty of time to spare.
#40: Get a scouting report of the opponents.
#41: When traveling to a race at altitude, start the race at a slower pace and arrive either at least two weeks before the race or as close as possible to the race.
#42: Warm up correctly before the race.
#43: Protect oneself in the heat.
#44: Control nerves at the starting line.
#45: Say something debilitating to an opponent at the starting line.
#46: Dress for success.
#47: Don't run a race on an empty stomach.
#48: Sleep.

Chapter 3: Winning During-Racing Strategies 61

#49: Run even or negative splits.
#50: Sit and kick.
#51: Surge.
#52: Stay close to an opponent at all times.
#53: Run fast up a hill.
#54: Run the first half to two thirds of the race with the head and the last third to half with the heart.
#55: Box in the opponent.
#56: Dictate the pace.
#57: Learn to react to opponents' moves.

#58: Be aggressive.

#59: Engage in self-talk.

#60: With one quarter to one half of a mile to go, be in the desired finishing place.

#61: Establish a rhythm early in the race.

#62: Focus and execute.

#63: Wear as little clothing as needed.

#64: Run the shortest path.

#65: Draft.

#66: Keep changing the pace.

#67: Count steps.

#68: Pass other runners with authority.

#69: Be strategic from behind.

#70: Be aware of the other runners.

#71: Never look back.

#72: Breathe rhythmically.

#73: Divide.

#74: Don't slow down.

#75: Use the other runners in the race to bring out the competitive animal inside.

#76: Draw on deeper emotions.

Chapter 4: Other Winning Racing Strategies 77

#77: Learn from past races.

#78: Know the *why* behind the *how*.

#79: Understand estrogen and what it can do for female runners.

#80: Always remain positive.

#81: Prevent injuries.

#82: Write down goals.

#83: Focus on the process rather than the outcome.

#84: Ask friends and family to watch the race.

#85: Wear the right shoes.

#86: Be a hero.

#87: Get educated.

#88: Become tough.

#89: Be patient.

#90: Eat a high carbohydrate diet.

#91: Drink chocolate milk immediately after workouts and races.

#92: Increase stride length.
#93: Own the process.
#94: Develop a personal definition of "winning."
#95: Don't race when fatigued.
#96: Don't race without the proper conditioning.
#97: Know strengths and weaknesses, and race to the strengths.
#98: Commit to being challenged.
#99: Don't do anything new on race day.
#100: Don't give away secrets.
#101: Learn the right moves.

About the Author 94

Introduction

When I was in high school, my electronics teacher had a silly, fortune cookie-type saying to remind his students of how to handle electrical wires: "One hand in pockey, no get shockey." Like touching wires with both hands, there's a wrong way to do almost everything. For example, going down a park slide head first, throwing a paper airplane at your high school teacher, and not buying your twin brother a birthday present, claiming you forgot his birthday, would all be considered by most as errors in judgment. (Okay, so I don't always make the best decisions.) Although racing errors won't have as severe a consequence as electrocuting yourself, understanding and employing specific strategies will make runners more successful racers. Most runners run races without giving much thought to how they are going to run the race. They just pay their entry fee and run, or run with their teammates, without any intention to their actions, hoping for a good result. Even the casual observer can often notice mistakes that cause a runner to have a bad race. Things like the weather, the competition, the race distance, anxiety, a runner's strengths and weaknesses, and the ability to execute a race plan all can affect the outcome of a race. Successful racing takes knowledge, planning, and execution. And a little courage. When runners train smart and effectively and they develop and execute a race plan, they'll achieve their potential and run winning races. That's why you need this book.

Ever since I ran my first race in elementary school as part of the Presidential Physical Fitness Test, I was hooked. The feeling of moving my arms and legs as fast as they could go to get from the start line to the finish line in the shortest time possible was so liberating and challenging and fun, I have made it my lifelong commitment to learn how to run winning races and how to get others to do so. Running a winning race doesn't necessarily mean finishing in first place. After all, only one person can finish first. Running a winning race means an athlete runs his *best* race, a race that he can be proud of, a race that he can walk away from feeling that he did the absolute best he could do on that day. Success should not always be measured by winning or by running fast; success should also be measured by an individual's ability to stand up to himself and his fears and his emotions and his hopes and improve his performance. And that's what *101 Winning Racing Strategies for Runners* is all about.

To guide runners in their endeavor to run winning races, *101 Winning Racing Strategies for Runners* is divided into themed chapters: Winning Training for Racing Strategies, Winning Pre-Racing Strategies, Winning During-Racing Strategies, and Other

Winning Racing Strategies. Runners may not be able to use every strategy for every race, so coaches and athletes should pick and choose what's appropriate for each unique situation and, over a racing career, try to incorporate as many strategies as possible.

Steve Prefontaine once remarked that a race is like a work of art that people can look at and be affected by in as many ways as they're capable of understanding. It is my hope that the winning racing strategies presented in this book will help runners run better, faster races and help them to create their own masterpiece.

1

Winning Training for Racing Strategies

#1: Train smarter.

Most runners don't train smartly. They do arbitrary workouts without having a systematic, progressive plan, and they do workouts at suboptimal speeds because they don't understand the purpose of the workouts. To train smarter, runners need to learn how to optimize their training and train at more effective levels of effort to get the best results. Smart training sets runners up for winning races. Although there are many paths to success when it comes to running, there are also wrong ways to train. For example, one of the biggest mistakes runners make is thinking that to run faster in races, they need to run faster in workouts. So they run their workouts faster than their current fitness level dictates. I once coached a college runner who ran around 19:00 for a cross-country 5K, and she told me she wanted to be trained like a 17:30 5K runner. So I told her to run a 17:30 5K, and then I'll train her like a 17:30 5K runner. Races, which demonstrate a runner's current level of fitness, dictate the training speeds, not the other way around. Unless a runner is a sprinter, distance runners don't do workouts to practice running faster. They do workouts to improve the physiological characteristics that will enable them to run faster in the future. Think of an assembly line: To make more products, the better strategy is to increase the number of workers (physiological characteristics) so as to have more assembly lines to do the work, rather than increase the speed at which the assembly line workers work. The goal of training is to obtain the greatest benefit while incurring the least amount of stress, so runners want to run as slow as possible while still obtaining the desired result.

#2: Train with a good coach.

Too many runners think they know it all when it comes to training. They coach themselves, picking workouts here and there that often don't conform to a plan. At best, their performances stay the same and they never meet their potential, and, at worst, they get injured. A knowledgeable coach is the greatest asset a runner can have. A good coach will design a seamless, progressive, systematic program and monitor what runners are doing. A coach relieves runners of the responsibility of planning their own training so they can focus on the training itself. Research shows that people who train under the supervision of a coach see better results than those who don't. While other runners and even many coaches can provide many workouts, it takes an expert to design workouts based on science, research, and experience that cause specific physiological changes and to organize the workouts into a progressive, systematic training program that allows runners to achieve optimum fitness and performance. Beyond that, a knowledgeable coach can also teach how to train most effectively and why to train a certain way. Knowing the how and why of training will go a long way toward becoming a more accomplished runner because it helps to develop an understanding of the process.

A coach will also prepare runners to race. He will advise on how to run races, discuss race strategy, and motivate and inspire runners to do things that they never thought possible. He can teach how to race effectively and help develop a race strategy to achieve the best result.

Having an outside pair of eyes is important. When trying to coach themselves, it's hard for runners to see things the way they really are since they're too close to the situation. Runners tend to always want to push themselves, thinking that constantly challenging themselves will lead to more success. Many runners want to run even when they are sick because they don't want to lose fitness and feel guilty by missing a run. Runners need a coach who can see the whole picture and determine when to push and when to back off and recover.

Runners should not underestimate the value of a good coach. A coach can be a trainer, motivator, teacher, a source of inspiration, and even a confidante. He can guide athletes to achieve a level of success that cannot be obtained on their own.

#3: Have a training plan.

As New York Yankees' catcher Yogi Berra once said, "If you don't know where you're going, you might not get there." Whether to run around the block or win a championship race, how runners train can have a dramatic effect on their performance. While running just to run may make a person fitter, training gives him the plan for success. It's the difference between building a house by placing bricks here and there and having a blueprint laid out beforehand. The training should not be arbitrary. A good training plan should work backwards from the goal race, with each phase of training planned out systematically. Rather than follow a generic plan, runners should use one that is skewed to their strengths. If their strength is endurance, they should focus more on mileage and tempo runs and less on interval training. If their strength is speed, they should focus less on mileage and more on interval training. Runners should work their strong points and train using the whole continuum of paces, from slow running speeds to very fast speeds to enhance both aerobic and anaerobic abilities.

#4: Run more.

The simplest, yet probably most effective, way to beat an opponent in a race is to run more than that opponent. To become a better distance runner, the number of miles run each week is the most important component of training.

Running lots of miles stimulates many physiological, biochemical, and molecular adaptations. One of the initial adaptations is an increase in blood volume. With a greater amount of blood circulating around the body comes a greater number of red blood cells, which transport oxygen. Inside the red blood cells is a protein called hemoglobin, which literally carries oxygen to the working muscles. These changes to the blood improve the blood vessels' ability to transport oxygen. Endurance training also stimulates the storage of more fuel (glycogen) in the muscles, increases the use of intramuscular fat to spare glycogen, creates a greater capillary network for a more rapid diffusion of oxygen into the muscles and, through the complex activation of gene expression, increases the muscles' mitochondrial density and the number of aerobic enzymes contained within them, increasing aerobic metabolic capacity. Mitochondria are very important since that is where aerobic metabolism takes place. They are like aerobic factories. The link between an increase in mitochondrial enzyme activity and an increase in mitochondria's capacity to consume oxygen, first made in 1967 in the muscles of rats, has provided much insight into the adaptability of skeletal muscle. Generally, the greater the demand, the greater the adaptations. In other words, the more athletes run, the more adaptations they'll make. But only up to a point. Unfortunately, the ability to adapt to a training stimulus doesn't keep occurring indefinitely. There will come a point, which is specific to each runner, when more training does not lead to more adaptations and faster race times. However, most runners run less than they could and, if they ran more, increasing their volume systematically and carefully so they don't get injured, would improve their performances and beat other runners in races.

#5: Improve running mechanics.

I see a lot of runners. And I see a lot of runners running badly. Many of these runners run races. Many of these runners get injured training for races. One of the reasons they get injured is because they haven't learned how to run before attempting to train for a race. It's like playing in a tennis tournament before learning how to hit a backhand. Or entering a golf tournament before learning how to swing a golf club. Or entering a triathlon before learning how to swim. Learning how to run correctly will help prevent injuries and enable runners to tolerate greater training loads since they will be undertaking the training with the proper skill to do so. To be a better runner, athletes need to start by running better.

For young and/or inexperienced runners who are still developing their running skills, drills that specifically target each part of the running motion can help improve running mechanics and coordination. Running has an underrecognized neural component. Just as the repetition of the walking movements decreases the jerkiness of a toddler's walk to the point that it becomes smooth, the repetition of specific running movements can make a runner smoother and improves running economy, the amount of oxygen used to maintain a given speed. Lots of extraneous movements, unnecessary muscle contractions, and an inefficient absorption of force at foot strike increase the use of oxygen to maintain a given speed, all of which make a runner uneconomical. Conversely, smooth, coordinated movements and the recruitment of the fewest muscle fibers needed for the task decreases the use of oxygen, which makes the runner economical. With countless repetitions, motor unit (muscle fiber) recruitment pattern becomes ingrained, allowing for smoother running mechanics and a more efficient application of muscular force. Once runners have learned and ingrained proper running mechanics, they will be better able to handle and even thrive off the training. In addition to the neural adaptation obtained with drills, drills can increase flexibility, since their dynamic action moves joints through an exaggerated range of motion.

When performing running drills, runners should take full recovery between each set and each drill to ensure the maintenance of proper form and avoid neuromuscular fatigue. They should be deliberate about all of the movements. Runners should remain either on the midfoot or the ball of the foot. It's better to not do the drills at all than to do them with improper form, since that will only create and ingrain bad habits. Like any other skill, these drills, and the proper running technique that they aim to produce, must be mastered before runners can train effectively and prepare to race. This cannot be emphasized enough. During all runs, it is vital to practice correct technique. It must become automatic. Runners must make a conscious effort to run as lightly as possible over the ground, feeling their feet land directly under the body and springing off the ground. They should not overstride by landing sharply with the heel and the leg out in front of the body. This will cause deceleration. Whether landing slightly on the heel first or on the midfoot is not as important as where the foot lands in relation to the body. The faster athletes run, the more they will naturally land toward the forefoot.

After practicing the drills a few times, runners should immediately follow each drill with strides for 50 meters to ingrain the movements into their running. They must practice these drills using crisp, sharp motions with a springiness to the legs.

High Knee Walk: This drill focuses on the hip flexors. Runners should march two to four sets of 30 meters, bringing the hip to 90 degrees so that the thighs are parallel to the ground. Focus should be kept on creating 90-degree angles at the knee and at the ankle. Legs should come down directly underneath the center of gravity and land on the midfoot. Runners should use quick, sharp movements.

High Knee Skip: This drill is similar to the high knee walk, but is performed as a skip, focusing on three 90-degree angles: hip, knee, and ankle. Legs should come down directly underneath the center of gravity and land on the midfoot. Runners should use quick, sharp movements. They should do two to four sets of 30 meters.

High Knee Run: This drill is similar to the high knee walk and skip, but is performed as a run. The horizontal distance is covered slowly, as the emphasis is on moving the legs up and down as fast as possible, like a piston or sewing machine. Runners should think of the ground as hot coals, picking the leg up as soon as it touches the ground. Legs should come down directly underneath the center of gravity. Runners should remain on the ball of the foot. They should run tall, not lean back, and use quick, sharp movements. Runners should do two to four sets of 30 meters.

Butt Kicks: This drill focuses on the hamstrings. Runners should run two to four sets of 30 meters, focusing on flexing the knees and flicking the back of the butt with the heels of the shoes. Emphasis is on moving the legs fast. Legs should come down directly underneath the center of gravity. Runners should remain on the ball of the foot, using quick, sharp movements. They should do two to four sets of 30 meters.

Running Leg Cycle: All of the former drills come into play in this drill, which takes the legs through the entire running cycle. Runners should lean against a fence or pole and, while standing in place, move the leg through the entire running cycle—starting with the foot on the ground, extending the leg at the hip and sweeping the leg back, bending the knee and pulling the knee to the front of the body until the hip is at 90 degrees (also creating 90-degree angles at the knee and ankle), then lowering the leg to the ground under the center of gravity, and repeat. They should think: "Land, push off, pull through; land, push off, pull through." They should do two to three sets of 20 reps with each leg.

Bounding: In an exaggerated running motion, runners should bound (which looks like a combination of running and jumping) forward from one leg to the other. They should do two to four sets of 40 to 50 meters.

Strides: Controlled sprints (about mile race pace effort) should be run for 50 to 150 meters. Runners should aim for a fast, smooth feeling. They shouldn't press to go fast; the sprints should not feel difficult. Rather, they should relax and focus on moving the legs fast to increase stride rate, and extending the legs behind from the hip to increase stride length. Runners should take as much time as needed between each one to feel recovered. The strides should be done on flat ground. Taking too little recovery and/or making the strides last more than about 25 seconds introduces a metabolic demand and defeats the neuromuscular purpose of doing them.

But what about the arms? Are they important? Of course the arms are important, because the arms balance the legs. As Isaac Newton taught, for every action there is an equal and opposite reaction. Quick, powerful arm movements mean quick, powerful leg movements. Move the arms the wrong way, and the legs will move the wrong way. So runners also need to pay attention to their arms. After practicing how to move the legs and how to land with the feet directly beneath the hips, runners can add the motion of the arms. They should hold the arms close to the body and swing them back and forth from the shoulder like a pendulum, with the forearms swinging at a slight angle toward the body rather than directly straight forward and backward like a robot. They should keep the elbows bent at 90 degrees or slightly less. They must not allow the arms to cross over the midline of the chest. They should keep the palms of the hands facing the body and cup the hands as if gently holding a potato chip. They must swing the arms with quick, compact movements. They should not lean forward from their hips. They must keep the torso as still as possible. The only things that should be moving are the arms and the legs. To run faster, runners can increase the cadence of their arms, but keep the movements controlled and compact.

#6: Improve aerobic base.

A base is something on top of which a structure is built. If the base is weak, the structure falls apart. If the base is strong, the structure will have greater stability and will be able to be built taller without risk of toppling over. For a runner, the base is aerobic fitness. The better the base of aerobic fitness, the more solid the runner will be, whether recreational, elite, or somewhere in between.

To run fast or to improve endurance, runners must spend a lot of time running slow. This may seem counterintuitive, but it's the volume of training that ultimately dictates performance capacity. In order to accomplish a large training volume, runners must perform most of their running at a relatively slow pace. Base building forms the basis of any distance runner's training program. Indeed, the number of miles (or the amount of time) run each week is the most important part of training. While increasing weekly running volume has the obvious benefit of improving endurance so as to run longer faster, it also improves running economy (the amount of oxygen used to run at a given pace), which is an often underrecognized parameter influencing running performance. When running a lot, the muscles' metabolic machinery needed to use oxygen is increased. The constant repetition of the running movements also has a very important neural effect, making the athlete a smoother runner. Running more also burns more calories, helping to lose weight, which further reduces the amount of oxygen needed to run at a given pace.

Training can be thought of as a pyramid, with the base of that pyramid being aerobic fitness level (see figure). The bigger that aerobic base, the higher the peak of the pyramid as the base pushes the peak up to a greater height. To improve running, the biggest difference in athletes' training from year to year must be the size of the base. Focusing on the peak of the pyramid by adding more speedwork or by trying to run workouts faster will never make runners as good as first focusing on the base. Aerobic fitness also affects recovery. Since recovery from faster running is an aerobic process, being more aerobically fit allows runners to recover faster both during the recovery periods of interval workouts and following each workout.

Since the duration of effort is one of the key factors that arouse the biological signal to elicit adaptations that will ultimately lead to improvements in running performance, the amount of time (or number of miles) spent running is more important than the pace at which athletes run. Therefore, runs should be easy enough to allow them to increase weekly mileage over time. Instead of running the same amount every day, some days should be longer than others. For example, if running 30 miles per week, it's better to alternate longer runs with shorter runs rather than run five miles per day six days per week. Some days should incorporate a little more stress, some days a little less.

So, how much mileage needs to be run to acquire an adequate aerobic base? The answer depends on a number of factors, including genetically-determined propensity to continually adapt to aerobic training, the amount of time available to run, the specific

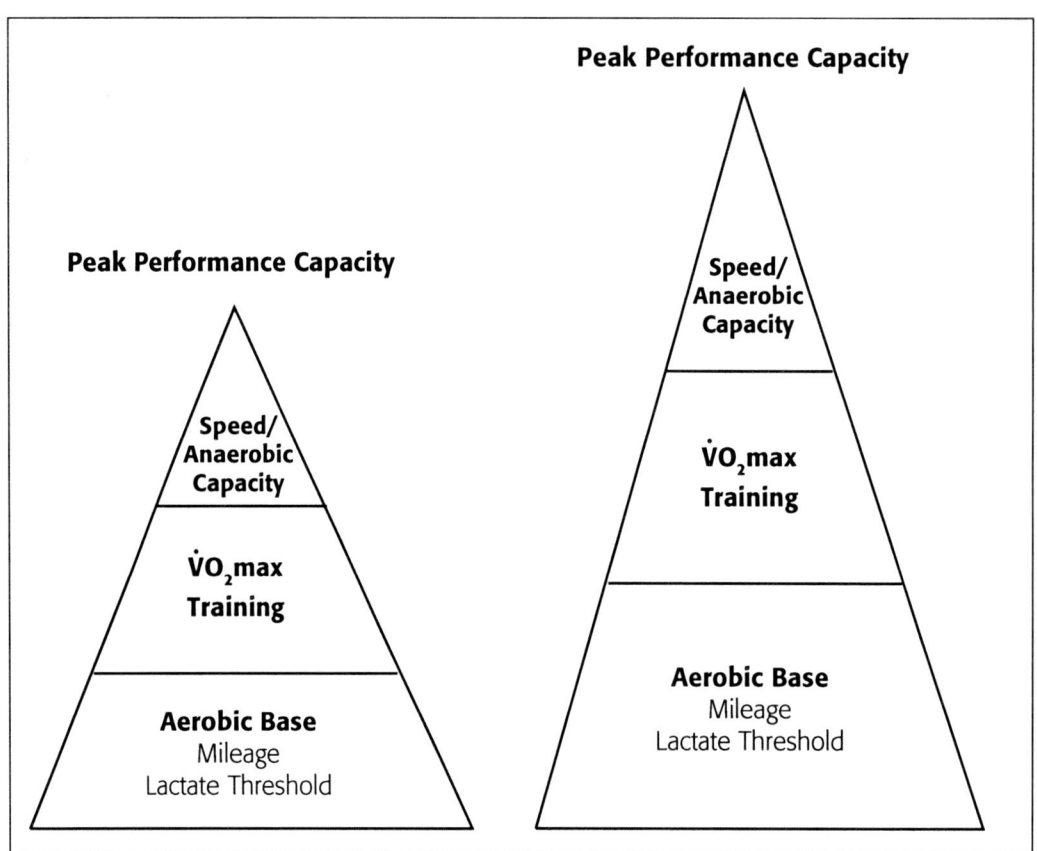

racing distance for which a person is training, and running goals (i.e., how good of a runner someone wants to be). Obviously, the longer the race for which athletes are training, the more mileage they need to run. Interestingly, however, there isn't a proportional relationship between weekly mileage and racing distance. In other words, if training for a half-marathon, athletes shouldn't expect to run half as much as when training for a marathon. Even though the marathon is twice as long as a half-marathon and more than four times as long as a 10K, marathon runners don't run double the weekly mileage as half-marathon runners and don't run four times as much as 10K runners. Even for shorter races, athletes need to run a lot. The best 5K runners in the world run almost as much as the best marathon runners. The reason for this is that any race that takes longer than three minutes to run is primarily influenced by the aerobic system. The shorter the race, the more critical anaerobic training becomes, but for all distance running races, aerobic metabolism is king.

The best way for runners to determine how much aerobic training is needed is to slowly and systematically increase mileage from month to month and year to year, taking care to note response to the training stimulus. When already running a lot (more than 40 miles per week), runners should not increase mileage unless prior training and racing experience gives reason to believe that improvement will continue with more mileage. If a plateau in performance hasn't been reached at 40 miles per week, there's no reason yet to increase the mileage to 50. Despite what many runners believe, more is not always better; more is only better if runners continue to adapt to more. If athletes haven't been running for very long, aerobic base building may be the only type of training to do for a while.

When working on building the aerobic base, runners should be careful when increasing mileage, since many runners get injured when increasing their weekly mileage, more so than when increasing their intensity. They should increase mileage by no more than one mile per day per week. For example, if currently running 20 miles in four days per week, athletes should run no more than 24 miles the next week by adding one mile to each of the four days. They should not run 24 miles the next week by adding all four miles to only one day of running. A highly-trained runner may be able to get away with adding more miles more quickly, especially if he has experience running more miles. New runners, older runners, or runners prone to injury should run the same mileage for three to four weeks before increasing it. They should give their legs a chance to adapt and habituate to each level of running before increasing the level. Whether running the same mileage for a few weeks or increasing the mileage slightly for a few weeks, they should back off the volume by about a third for one recovery week before increasing the training load. For example, if runners have been running 30 miles per week for three weeks, they should back off to 20 miles for one week before increasing above 30 miles for the next week. Think of this strategy as taking one step back at the end of each training cycle so as to take two steps forward during the next one. Over time, weekly mileage progression will look like the following:

- Weeks 1-4: 30-30-30-20 miles
- Weeks 5-8: 35-35-35-23 miles
- Weeks 9-12: 40-40-40-26 miles

The weekly mileage increases over time, but it is done systematically, which is the key for adaptation and preventing injuries.

Given the importance of aerobic development to running success, the aerobic base phase should be the longest phase of a training program. It takes longer to develop endurance than to develop speed. Depending on the starting point and running goals, runners may want to devote eight weeks (experienced) to 16 weeks (beginner) to their aerobic base. When training for a marathon and having never run before, runners may want to spend an entire year on the aerobic base.

Running a lot can make runners fatigued. When increasing mileage, they must make sure to get adequate recovery. Interestingly, all adaptations from training occur during the recovery from training, not during the training itself. The older runners are, the more time they need to recover from training, so the longer they need before increasing the volume. While young runners can get away with training mistakes because they recover quickly from high training loads, older runners must be more careful with how and when they increase their training loads.

#7: Improve acidosis threshold speed.

One of the main determinants of how fast athletes run any race is the speed at which their acidosis (lactate) threshold occurs. That's because the acidosis threshold represents the fastest speed that can be sustained aerobically. Historically referred to as the lactate threshold because its presence is detected when lactate accumulates in the blood, the real physiological marker of interest is the acidosis rather than the lactate since it is the acidosis, rather than the lactate, that contributes to fatigue. This threshold demarcates the transition between aerobic running and running that includes a significant contribution from oxygen-independent (anaerobic) metabolism. Training the acidosis threshold increases the speed at which acidosis occurs, enabling athletes to run at a faster pace before they fatigue because they'll be running faster before oxygen-independent metabolism begins to play a significant role. The benefit to being able to run aerobically at 6:30 pace compared to 7:00 pace is obvious: it means athletes will be running 30 seconds per mile faster before they fatigue. Opponents will never be able to keep up.

The acidosis threshold can be targeted by running at or near acidosis threshold pace. Acidosis threshold pace is about 10 to 15 seconds per mile slower than 5K race pace (or about 10K race pace) for runners slower than about 40 minutes for 10K. If using a heart rate (HR) monitor, the pace is about 80 to 85 percent maximum HR. For highly trained and competitive runners, acidosis threshold pace is about 25 to 30 seconds per mile slower than 5K race pace (or about 15 to 20 seconds per mile slower than 10K race pace) and corresponds to about 85 to 90 percent max HR. Subjectively, the pace feels comfortably hard. Runners can choose from these five types of acidosis threshold (AT) workouts:

- *AT Run:* Continuous run at AT pace, starting at about 3 miles (15 to 20 minutes) and increasing up to 5 to 6 miles (about 45 minutes). This is the most basic of AT workouts, but it is very effective for improving acidosis threshold. It's important to keep the AT pace as steady as possible during this workout, with little to no fluctuation in pace. The point is to raise blood lactate level to its threshold value (which indicates the onset of acidosis), and then hold it there for the duration of the workout.
- *Long AT Run:* For marathoners who need to get used to running for longer periods of time at close to AT pace, this workout is a continuous run slightly slower than AT pace, such as 6 to 10 miles (45 to 60 minutes) at 10 to 20 seconds per mile slower than AT pace. Sometimes, it's beneficial to run a bit slower than AT pace to accommodate a longer distance, which comes with it the psychological demand of holding a comfortably hard pace for an extended time.
- *AT Intervals:* Short runs at AT pace with short rest intervals, such as 4 x 1 mile at AT pace with 1 minute rest or 8 x 1,000 meters at AT pace with 1 minute rest. This interval workout makes the AT run both physically and psychologically easier and increases the distance athletes can run at AT pace. While it is tempting to run faster

when the work periods are shorter, the purpose of this workout is the same as it is with the continuous AT run: to increase the acidosis threshold. Therefore, runners should make sure not to run any faster when doing AT intervals as when doing AT runs. They should still run at AT pace. Each repetition should be run at exactly the same pace, completing all reps within as close as possible a time to each other.

- *AT+ Intervals:* This version of AT intervals is run slightly faster than AT pace (hence the plus) with very short rest intervals, such as two sets of 3 to 4 x 800 to 1,000 meters at 5 to 10 seconds per mile faster than AT pace with 45 seconds rest and two minutes rest between sets. This workout, performed after completing a number of AT runs and AT intervals, adds slightly more stress to the AT intervals as a way to further stimulate changes in AT pace to reach a faster speed.
- *AT/LSD Combo Run:* A twist on the 1970s term "long slow distance," this challenging workout for marathoners is a medium- to long-distance run (12 to 16 miles) with a portion at AT pace, such as 4 miles at AT pace + 8 miles easy; 5 miles easy + 3 miles at AT pace + 5 miles easy + 3 miles at AT pace; and 10 miles easy + 4 miles at AT pace.

#8: Spend time running at faster speeds.

Many runners only go on slow runs, staying away from speedwork. While easy, aerobic running is the basis of a training program, athletes can't run slow all the time. Running slow all the time will just make a slow runner. Once runners have a solid aerobic base of miles behind them, they need to incorporate faster workouts into their training program. Train using the whole continuum of paces, from slow running speeds to very fast speeds to enhance both aerobic and anaerobic abilities. Fartleks, acidosis threshold runs, intervals, and hill sprints all can help runners learn a range of speeds and get faster.

#9: Increase $\dot{V}O_2$max.

$\dot{V}O_2$max is the maximum volume of oxygen that muscles consume per minute. It is, therefore, referred to as *aerobic power* since it's a measure of the *rate* at which oxygen is consumed.

$\dot{V}O_2$max is the best single indicator of a person's aerobic fitness. Although a high $\dot{V}O_2$max alone is not enough to attain great performances, it gains runners access into the club. Runners simply cannot attain a high level of performance without a high $\dot{V}O_2$max. It is especially important for the middle distances (800 meters to 2 miles), races that are run at or close to 100 percent $\dot{V}O_2$max.

$\dot{V}O_2$max is dependent on central factors, such as cardiac output and blood flow to the muscles, and peripheral factors, such as oxygen extraction and use by the muscles. Cardiac output, the amount of blood pumped by the left ventricle of the heart per minute, is dependent on stroke volume and heart rate. Stroke volume, the amount of blood pumped by the left ventricle of the heart per beat, is determined by the return of blood back to the heart through the venous circulation (venous return), the heart's ability to contract quickly and forcefully, the amount of pressure in the left ventricle (preload) and in the aorta (afterload), and the size of left ventricle. How much oxygen can be extracted and used by the muscles is dependent on mitochondrial and capillary volumes. The more capillaries that perfuse the muscle fibers, the shorter the diffusion distance for oxygen from the capillaries to the mitochondria, microscopic energy factories that contain the enzymes involved in aerobic metabolism. The number of enzymes is also important, since enzymes, through their effect on chemical reactions, control metabolism. Oxygen extraction is reflected by the difference in the amount of oxygen going to the muscles through the *arterial* circulation and the amount coming out through the *venous* circulation (a-v O_2 difference). The a-v O_2 difference is determined by the convection of oxygen through the muscle capillaries and its diffusion from the capillaries to the mitochondria. Runners who can shift most of the blood from inactive tissues to the active muscles will have a large a-v O_2 difference because the active muscles will extract more oxygen from the blood than will the inactive tissues. Since the amount of oxygen in the arterial circulation is the same at rest as it is during a race, any change in the a-v O_2 difference is a result of a decrease in oxygen in the venous circulation, which means the muscles have extracted more oxygen.

$\dot{V}O_2$ is equal to the product of the central and peripheral factors:

$$\dot{V}O_2 = SV \times HR \times (\text{a-v } O_2 \text{ difference})$$

Since SV x HR equals cardiac output (CO), the equation can be written as:

$$\dot{V}O_2 = CO \times (\text{a-v } O_2 \text{ difference})$$

$\dot{V}O_2$max occurs when SV, HR (and therefore CO), and the a-v O_2 difference are all at their maximum, which means runners have to be running hard.

While unfit people seem to be equally limited by central and peripheral factors (they lack both a high blood flow and abundant metabolic machinery), trained runners seem to be more centrally limited. Training appears to result in a shift of the limitation on the sliding scale; the more fit runners become, the more they move away from a metabolic limitation to $\dot{V}O_2$max and the closer they move to an oxygen supply limitation. Progressive increases in mileage from month to month and year to year will improve $\dot{V}O_2$max by increasing the muscles' metabolic capacity. When runners have achieved a high level of mileage, the intensity of training becomes more important to increase the cardiac factors responsible for maximizing oxygen supply to the muscles.

While $\dot{V}O_2$max can initially be improved by increasing weekly running mileage, it is best improved with interval workouts, with the work periods lasting 3 to 5 minutes. During the work periods, athletes should run at or very close to $\dot{V}O_2$max. Repeatedly reaching and sustaining $\dot{V}O_2$max during the work periods represents the stimulus for its improvement. If the recovery period is short (equal to or less than the time spent running), oxygen consumption ($\dot{V}O_2$) will not decrease all the way back down to its resting value. This is a good thing, because the next work period will then begin with the $\dot{V}O_2$ elevated. $\dot{V}O_2$ will then rise again during the subsequent work period, to a point higher than during the first work period. If planned right, $\dot{V}O_2$ will reach $\dot{V}O_2$max after a couple of work periods, which is the goal of the workout. These workouts are difficult, as not only is oxygen being consumed at its fastest rate, but there is also a considerable oxygen-independent (anaerobic) contribution to the workout. $\dot{V}O_2$max pace is equal to one- to one-and-a-half-mile race pace for recreational runners and 3,000-meter or two-mile race pace for highly trained and competitive runners. Runners should come close to reaching their maximum heart rate by the end of each work period. Sample $\dot{V}O_2$max workouts include:

- 3-4 x 1,200 meters at $\dot{V}O_2$max pace with a 1:≤1 work:rest ratio
- 5-6 x 1,000 meters at $\dot{V}O_2$max pace with a 1:≤1 work:rest ratio
- 6-8 x 800 meters at $\dot{V}O_2$max pace with a 1:≤1 work:rest ratio
- 16-20 x 400 meters $\dot{V}O_2$max pace with a 1:<1 work:rest ratio

While longer work periods provide a greater load on the cardiovascular system, an advantage of shorter work periods is that runners can perform a greater volume of work at $\dot{V}O_2$max pace by breaking the work up into smaller segments. Although it can be tempting to run faster when the work periods are shorter, athletes should run at the same pace for all $\dot{V}O_2$max interval workouts regardless of the length of the work periods they choose since the goal is the same: to increase $\dot{V}O_2$max. As they progress, runners should make the workouts harder by adding more reps or decreasing the recovery intervals rather than by running faster. They should only increase the speed of the work periods once races have shown that fitness has improved.

#10: Increase anaerobic capacity.

In addition to the large aerobic contribution to distance running races, there is also a significant involvement of anaerobic metabolism in races shorter than 10K, since the races are run at a speed faster than the acidosis threshold for most runners. When running faster than the heart and blood flow can provide oxygen to the muscles, some of the energy for muscle contraction is regenerated through anaerobic, or "oxygen-independent," means. When this happens, a number of problems begin to arise inside runners' muscles. Primary among them is that the muscles lose their ability to contract effectively because of an increase in hydrogen ions, which causes the muscle pH to decrease, a condition called acidosis. Acidosis has a number of side effects: it inhibits the enzyme that breaks down the energy molecule (ATP) inside muscles, which decreases muscle contractile force; it inhibits the release of calcium (the trigger for muscle contraction) from its storage site in muscles; and it inhibits the production of ATP from the metabolic pathway glycolysis by inhibiting glycolysis' most important enzyme.

In addition to hydrogen ion accumulation, other metabolites accumulate when running fast, including inorganic phosphate (P_i), ADP, and potassium, each of which causes a specific problem inside muscles, from inhibition of specific enzymes involved in muscle contraction to interference with muscles' electrical charges, ultimately leading to a decrease in muscle force production and running speed.

Given the many fatigue-inducing factors associated with oxygen-independent metabolism, it's important for runners to develop anaerobic capacity once they have developed themselves as aerobically as possible. The purposes of anaerobic capacity training are to cause a high degree of muscle acidosis to enhance buffering capacity, to increase the number of enzymes that catalyze the chemical reactions in anaerobic glycolysis (the energy system that breaks down blood glucose and muscle and liver glycogen to resynthesize ATP) so that glycolysis can regenerate ATP more quickly for muscle contraction, and to increase running speed by recruiting fast-twitch muscle fibers.

To improve anaerobic capacity, athletes can run 45-second to two-minute repeats with recovery intervals one to three times as long as the time spent running. They should run fast enough to cause acidosis and recruit fast-twitch muscle fibers—400-meter race pace for recreational runners and 800-meter to mile race pace for competitive runners. Sample anaerobic capacity workouts include:

- 6 to 8 x 400 meters at mile race pace with a 1:1 work:rest ratio
- Two sets of 400/800/400 meters at mile race pace with 1 minute recovery and 5 minutes recovery between sets
- Two sets of 4 x 300 meters at 800-meter race pace with a 1:2 work:rest ratio and 5 minutes recovery between sets

#11: Maximize recovery.

Recovery may be the most overlooked aspect of training. Most runners focus on how many miles and what pace to run. Improvements in fitness, however, occur during the *recovery* period between training sessions, not during the training itself. Positive physiological adaptations to training occur when a correctly-timed alternation occurs between stress and recovery. When finishing a workout, runners are weaker, not stronger. How much weaker depends on the intensity and duration of the workout. If the stress is too great and/or recovery is not complete before the next workout or race, performance and ability to adapt to subsequent training sessions will decline. The faster and more complete the recovery, the more runners will get out of training and the more prepared they will be to race. Therefore, runners must be recovered from a workout to fully benefit from the next one and they must be recovered from training to be fully prepared for a race. The most effective adaptations occur when runners are recovered from previous training and best prepared to tolerate a subsequent overload. People can't train hard all the time. Periodic decreases in training load give the body time to adapt to the training stress and allow accumulated fatigue to diminish, making athletes ready for a higher load of training. How much or how long to back off depends on the severity of the training load, the level of fatigue, and the distance of the upcoming race. Usually a week is sufficient, with a longer recovery for longer races. The key is to be as fresh as possible for the race without having lost any fitness. A number of factors affect how quickly and completely runners recover from their workouts, including age, training intensity, nutrition, environment, stress, and level of cardiovascular fitness. The most significant of these factors is age, as younger runners recover faster between workouts, enabling them to perform hard workouts more often. Workout intensity is the next biggest factor, with higher intensity workouts requiring longer recovery time. Environment also plays a role in recovery, with altitude and cold weather slowing recovery. Since recovery is an aerobic process, a high level of cardiovascular fitness speeds recovery due to the quicker delivery of nutrients and removal of metabolic waste by the circulatory system.

#12: Get more powerful muscles.

At first glance, distance running doesn't seem to have much to do with big, powerful muscles. Indeed, the best distance runners in the world are quite small, with slim legs and arms. However, athletes can still benefit from power training as a distance runner, as long as they don't start looking like a sprinter or bodybuilder. It's not what muscles look like; it's what they do that matters.

Power, one of the most overlooked traits for endurance performance, is the product of muscular force (strength) and velocity (speed). Strength is the maximum amount of force muscles produce, and is dependent on muscle size, type of muscle fibers, and movement speed, among other factors. While being strong is important, the feet are in contact with the ground for too short of a time while running to produce maximum force. It is far more important to produce force as quickly as possible. An insightful strategy to become a faster runner is to enhance the steps involved in muscle fiber recruitment and contraction, improving the speed at which muscles produce force.

Muscular power can be improved by using maximum and explosive strength training (e.g., three to four sets of five to six repetitions at greater than 85 percent of one-rep max), which focuses on the strength component of power, and sprint and plyometric training (ballistic jumping and bounding exercises involving repeated rapid eccentric (lengthening) and concentric (shortening) muscle contractions), which focus on the speed component of power. Both heavy strength training and sprint/plyometric training increase the central nervous system's ability to recruit muscle fibers quickly. In addition to improving the speed at which muscles produce force, power training can improve running economy (the oxygen cost of maintaining a specific speed) through its effects on neuromuscular factors. Therefore, when training for muscular strength, the resistance must be heavy enough with few repetitions so as to not increase muscle size (hypertrophy), as doing so would reduce running economy by adding body mass.

#13: Train with others.

Much has been written about the loneliness of the long-distance runner. Although running alone has its perks and offers a chance—maybe the only one all day—to be alone, sometimes it helps to train with others. After all, humans are social animals.

Training with others, especially if they are of equal or a slightly greater performance level, makes workouts easier by having other runners to help with the work. Athletes can become faster since other runners can push them and bring things out in them that are hard to bring out individually. Other runners also offer motivation, encouragement, camaraderie, and accountability. There's a reason why the best runners train with other runners rather than by themselves.

#14: Understand adaptation, and train progressively.

While runners often hear about training and adaptation, how does that adaptation occur? How much runners adapt to a training stimulus ultimately depends on how responsive their cells are to signals. Muscle cells are able to detect all kinds of signals—mechanical, metabolic, neural, and hormonal, which are amplified and transmitted via signaling cascades and lead to the events involved in gene expression. This signaling is fast, occurring within minutes of completing a workout. Signaling results in the activation of transcription factors, which are proteins that bind to a specific part of DNA and control the transfer of genetic information from DNA to RNA.

Many of the physiological and biochemical adaptations to training begin with DNA, with the copying of one of its double helical strands (a process called replication). The replicated DNA strand, under the action of transcription factors, is then transcribed into messenger RNA (a process called transcription), and the messenger RNA is then translated into a protein (a process called translation). Finally, the protein is transported from the nucleus of the cell where transcription and translation occur to the place where it will function.

While a single workout alone, especially if it is new, introduces a specific signal and activation of transcription factors, repeated workouts lead to a concerted accumulation of messenger RNAs that can be translated into a host of structural and functional proteins. In the case of distance running, the accumulation of proteins is manifested, for example, as an increase in the number of mitochondria, the microscopic aerobic factories responsible for aerobic metabolism.

When beginning a training program, runners will experience many signaling responses and subsequent adaptations. However, continual training at the same level decreases the training-specific signaling responses involved in the adaptations to training. In other words, if training stays the same, runners can expect performances to stay the same. For example, if an athlete runs 10 miles on Sunday morning when he is used to running only 8, a strong signal will be sent to make specific adaptations (e.g., an increase in mitochondria, muscle glycogen content, etc.). If the athlete continues to run 10 miles every Sunday for a period of time, he will continue to send signals to make adaptations until those adaptations are fully realized. After running 10 miles so many times that he has become habituated to it, a 10-mile run will no longer be enough of a stimulus to initiate any further adaptations. Therefore, to force more adaptations, the athlete must run longer than 10 miles (or run the miles faster). To become a better runner and run faster races, an athlete must gradually, systematically, and progressively increase the amount of stress to increase the signaling response and subsequent adaptations.

#15: Taper training before important races.

I attended a high school that was known for its swimmers. They were the best in the country, and some of them competed in the Olympics. Before championship meets, you could overhear amusing discussions in the hallways about "shaving down" and "tapering" in an attempt to swim faster. As a member of the cross country and track teams, I was also interested in getting faster. So I couldn't help but eavesdrop. "What were these odd-sounding things?" I wondered. "Could they work for me, too? Do swimmers have a secret?"

The idea of tapering the training load has been a long tradition among swimmers, the most often-studied athletes in regard to tapering. While it's not necessary as a runner to shave all body hair to run faster, runners can benefit from tapering their training. Since most runners are a driven bunch, it seems unnatural to cut weekly running volume to a fraction of current training. Competitive runners think they should always do more. When tapering training, however, the body is provided the opportunity to recover, adapt, and overcompensate to the training to be prepared to run the best race.

Most research on runners, swimmers, and cyclists has shown that improved performance (from 0.5 to 6 percent) is more likely to occur after a period of tapering. Among the most prominent physiological changes that occur during the taper are in the characteristics of the blood, including increases in red blood cell volume, total blood volume, and reticulocytes (immature red blood cells), and improvements in the health of red blood cells. These hematological changes reflect a positive balance between hemolyis (the degradation of red blood cells) and erythropoiesis (the production of red blood cells), leading to a greater oxygen carrying capability and, often, an improved performance.

Tapering also increases muscle glycogen content (providing more fuel), aerobic enzyme activity (allowing for greater aerobic metabolism), and muscular strength and power, and increases or maintains maximum oxygen consumption ($\dot{V}O_2$max). There is also a decreased level of the enzyme creatine kinase in the blood (an indirect indicator of muscle damage), which reflects an increased recovery.

The goal of tapering is to recover from prior training without compromising previous training adaptations. In other words, runners want to decrease fatigue without losing fitness. Unfortunately, research has not clearly established the time frame separating the benefits of a successful taper from the negative consequences of insufficient training, leaving most runners and coaches to take a trial-and-error approach. Studies on tapering in runners have only used one-week tapers and have not examined the taper's effects on long-distance running performance. Typically, the longer the race, the longer the taper. The exact duration of a taper will vary depending on prior training load, level of fatigue, and genetically-predetermined ability to retain training effects while reducing the training stimulus (i.e., how quickly a runner loses fitness). If runners tend to fall out of shape fast, they don't want a long taper. Positive physiological adaptations and performance gains have been found using tapers lasting six to seven days in university-aged runners, 4 to 14 days in cyclists and triathletes, and 10 days in strength-trained athletes. Masters runners (over age 40) who take longer to recover from hard training may need to taper for longer than one week.

Runners should reduce their weekly mileage exponentially for one to two weeks (two to four weeks for the marathon) but maintain training intensity with interval training (if they've already been doing so pre-taper). As the race gets closer, they need to reduce the volume of intensity by reducing the number of intervals in each session. Research has shown that reductions in training volume up to 60 to 90 percent can improve performance, however the research is limited to short races. Decreasing mileage by as much as 90 percent would not be recommended for long races like the half-marathon and marathon given their large dependence on aerobic capacity.

Exactly what runners do during their taper will depend on what they did before the taper. They shouldn't introduce any new workouts during the taper, as that would only cause fatigue. While tapering has become in vogue, runners should remember that it is not a magic bullet. Tapering without a heavy training load preceding it won't do much. The more training done prior to the taper, the greater the effect the taper will have on racing performance.

#16: Become very familiar with what different paces feel like.

One of the keys to successful racing is to become intimately familiar with different paces. Developing an internal clock can prevent runners from starting races too fast and make them more aware of what they're doing in the race rather than just throwing caution to the wind and hoping for the best. Proper pacing is vital for success in most races, becoming more important the longer the race. In the marathon, for example, deviating from an average race pace by more than two percent is metabolically more costly than remaining within that range.

In learning what different paces feel like, runners want to get to the point that if someone were to say to them, "Run at 5K race pace," they are able to run at 5K race pace without looking at a watch. To accomplish this, I sometimes take my athletes' watches away from them when they run workouts on the track and give them feedback only from my stopwatch every lap so they can learn the pace of the workout. Runners should use workouts to learn a sense of pace. Tracks are invaluable for this. When doing a workout on the track, runners can monitor the pace every 100 meters since tracks are marked in 100-meter segments. If not good at pacing, runners can calculate the pace of their workout for every 100 meters and look at their watch at each marking. They should make adjustments to the pace if they're too fast or too slow. After having done that for a few workouts, they can look at their watch every 200 meters, then every 300 meters, and then every 400 meters. For longer races like the marathon, some of the runs can be done on marked paths, working up to looking at the watch every other mile. Over time, runners should be able to acquire a keen sense of pacing as they "feel" the workouts.

#17: Periodize training.

Runners love routine. They run the same routes and the same paces day after day. However, if they want to become better runners and run winning races, they need to vary the training stimulus. Periodization, which began in Europe in the 1910s in response to the need to vary the training of athletes who were beginning to train year-long, is a method of maximizing fitness and performance by structuring training programs into periods or phases, using programmed variation of training loads and recovery in a cyclic fashion. It involves focusing the training stimulus to one or two variables at a time and manipulating and systematically changing those training variables over the course of the training program. By varying the training, the stimulus is changed so the runners continue to adapt. For example, instead of running 30 minutes easy every day of the week, runners can vary and polarize training so that some days of the week they run more than 30 minutes and some days they run less, and some days they run very hard and some days they run very easy. Training using a programmed variation of volume and intensity produces better results compared to training without variation. While variation is vital to preventing plateaus, all changes to a training program should be made with concrete training goals in mind and never on a strictly random basis for the sheer sake of variety. The training emphases and sequencing should be guided by the runners' strengths and weaknesses, spending more time on aspects of fitness that attend to their strengths.

There are a few different ways to schedule and organize the variation of training stimuli. The traditional way is called linear periodization, during which the training program initially builds in volume before decreasing in volume and increasing in intensity. The opposite structure, reverse linear periodization, begins with higher intensity and progresses to lower intensity and higher volume. Finally, with non-linear (or undulating) periodization, the volume and intensity change from week to week or even from day to day throughout the program. Research on periodization, which is limited to strength training, has shown that all three of these models of periodization are effective for increasing muscular strength and altering body composition; however, distance running favors linear periodization due to the benefits that come from initially establishing a strong aerobic base.

To periodize training, runners should initially build their aerobic base by increasing the volume of running each week and each month. Every three to four weeks during this aerobic build-up, they should drop the volume by about a third for one recovery week. Decreasing the training load, while considered egregious by most competitive runners, is important because it allows the body to absorb the training provided and make the necessary adaptations that will enable them to run faster. It also functions as an active recovery period from the training, preparing runners to handle the greater training load to come. After they have reached a significant amount of mileage (different for each runner depending on goals, time and commitment to train, and race distance for which they're training), runners should either maintain the volume or decrease it slightly and increase the intensity by doing more quality workouts, such as acidosis threshold runs and interval workouts. Finally, they should drop the volume dramatically and increase the intensity with speedwork. This training design will make runners sharp for their race. While this linear periodization design is most commonly used for distance runners, there cannot be one periodization model since there is a large inter-individual response to training, both in magnitude of response and time frame for developing and retaining training effects. Thus, how the different training components are organized and how the volume and intensity are manipulated is an individual matter.

Periodization is also a smart way to rehabilitate an injury. At a time when the balancing act of training enough to stimulate maintenance or gains in fitness but not training too much as to delay healing or cause reinjury is of utmost importance, runners need to be extra careful when increasing their training. Since the injured body part is weaker than normal, increasing the training load too much too soon will prevent them from getting over the injury and may even cause a reinjury. Doing too much too soon is the main reason why people become injured in the first place. By periodizing the rehabilitation program, runners can slowly and systematically introduce greater and greater stimuli, allowing enough time for the injured body part to adapt to each new stimulus. For example, a fractured bone will heal stronger when asked to bear weight (following a significant period of complete rest); however, placing too much weight on the bone can prolong the healing process and actually cause it to be reinjured. Since the human body adapts quite well to a stress that is applied in small doses, periodization is an elegant and effective way to return from an injury.

#18: Practice running hills.

Off the track, hills are often a part of racing, which means runners have to learn how to run hills. When running uphill, they should exaggerate arm swing, lean into the hill, and push off with the ball of the foot to drive themselves up the hill. They should aim for a specific effort rather than a specific speed since running uphill uncouples the effort from the speed (i.e., they're running relatively slowly even though they're working hard). Runners shouldn't try to fight gravity and pick up the pace on a hill. The hills can be used to maintain the momentum that was set prior to the hills. At the top of each hill, runners should focus on opening their stride, which has shortened on the hill, and cresting the top. It's easy for runners to slow down once they reach the top of a hill because they're fatigued. So that's a good place to pick up the pace slightly and pull away from opponents.

When running downhill, runners should shorten their stride to prevent overstriding and focus on moving the legs quickly, which will keep momentum going forward. Since runners can run pretty fast downhill because gravity is pulling them, there is less time to decide on foot placement, so they must look ahead a few steps to prepare.

Even though running uphill seems harder, as the heart feels like it's about to burst out of the chest, downhills cause the biggest problems. The reason downhills are so tough is because of the gravity-induced eccentric muscle contractions, during which muscle fibers are forced to lengthen, causing microscopic tears. The forces of impact and braking are also greater during downhill running. All of this muscle damage makes the muscles less capable of producing force, which can slow the pace. A winning racing strategy for races that have downhill sections is to cause that damage in training because damaging muscle fibers with eccentric contractions makes them heal back stronger, protecting them from future damage. While runners can expect their muscles to be sore after the first time running downhill, subsequent downhill runs will cause less soreness since running downhill has a prophylactic effect on muscle damage and soreness.

#19: Run time trials.

Time trials are a great way to determine fitness level and build confidence in a relaxed, non-pressure situation. When run with other people, they can also provide an opportunity to practice a race. When preparing for a race shorter than 10K, runners can do one half to two thirds of the upcoming racing distance as fast as possible or at some percentage of maximum speed. Low-key races can also be used as time trials.

#20: Develop a finishing kick.

Many races come down to the final sprint at the end, whether trying to win the race or running in the middle of the pack and just trying to beat a best friend. The last thing runners want is to get passed in the final 200 meters of a race. It doesn't feel good. Runners should spend some time in training developing a strong finishing kick. To develop the kick, the following workouts can be helpful:

- Run 3 to 4 x 800 to 1,000 meters at 3K (2-mile) race pace + 4 to 6 x 400 meters at mile race pace with a 1:1 work:rest ratio during the 800/1,000-meter portion of the workout and a 1:2 work:rest ratio during the 400-meter portion of the workout. For example, a runner who can run 5K in 17:00 should run 3 to 4 x 1,000 meters in 3:16 to 3:19 (5:14 to 5:19 pace) with 3:15 jog recovery + 4 to 6 x 400 meters in 73 to 74 seconds (4:54 pace) with 2:25 jog recovery.
- Run at the racing distance (5K to 10K) at acidosis threshold pace or slightly faster in a group of runners with similar abilities, with one runner being designated as the kicker (with only the coach and the kicker knowing who the kicker is). The kicker starts the kick at a pre-planned place on the course (far enough out from the finish to serve the purpose of an early kick). When the kicker kicks, it's his job to pull away from the pack and each of the other runners' job to try to stay with the kicker. To more closely simulate kicking off of race pace, runners can run at race pace instead of acidosis threshold pace, with the distance of the run shortened from the racing distance. The kicker shouldn't simply sprint away from everyone in the last 100 meters. This workout is about developing a kick that can begin as early as can be held, so it's better to run at 90 percent for 600 meters than 100 percent for 100 meters.

#21: Use interval training wisely.

Every high school track coach in the country knows that the fastest way to get athletes in shape is interval training. In the 1960s, famous Swedish physiologist Per-Olaf Åstrand discovered, using a stationary bicycle in a laboratory, what many coaches and runners already knew: that by breaking up a set amount of work into smaller segments, a greater volume of work can be performed at a higher intensity. Sounds obvious, but Åstrand's simple observation is the basis for interval training and the basis for improving fitness quickly. Research shows that, to improve or maintain fitness, the intensity of training is more important than either the volume (i.e., weekly mileage) or the frequency (i.e., number of days per week).

While interval training can make runners faster, any short-term success may likely occur to the detriment of long-term development and consistency of performances. It can also bring athletes to a premature peak if they use it too soon and can significantly increase chance of injury. If runners hold off on the interval training until they have developed themselves as aerobically as possible, they will ultimately get more from interval training when it is time to do it.

The other issue concerning interval training is how it is used. It is not used to run athletes into the ground. They should be tired but not completely spent after an interval workout. Remember, the purpose of interval training is to perform a greater volume of work at a higher intensity compared to what they can perform if they were to run the distance continuously. The purpose is not to run so fast for so many repetitions that they can't walk off the track. Runners want to finish the workout feeling like they are in control, like they could have squeezed out another repetition.

#22: When training for a marathon, don't consume carbohydrates during long training runs.

Scientists first discovered in the 1960s that the ability to contract muscles for prolonged periods is strongly influenced by the amount of carbohydrate stored in skeletal muscles (glycogen), with muscle glycogen depletion becoming the decisive factor limiting prolonged exercise. Most runners have enough glycogen to provide energy for only about 70 minutes of running. Even with the contribution of fat helping to delay the depletion of glycogen, moderate-intensity running can only be sustained for two to three hours.

When athletes run out of carbohydrates, muscles are forced to rely on fat and consequently the pace slows down because the muscles regenerate energy slower when using fat compared to when using carbohydrates. To compensate for a lack of carbohydrates, the liver, sensing the carbohydrate fuel tank is getting low, synthesizes glucose from non-carbohydrate sources, namely amino acids and lactate.

With the popularity of marathon running has also come the popularity of carbohydrate drinks, gels, and bars to replenish blood glucose while running. It seems that everyone now does Sunday long runs with a fuel belt around their waists. While ingesting carbohydrates during long runs may allow runners to feel better since they'll maintain blood glucose levels, it defeats the purpose of the run, which is to deplete carbohydrates so specific adaptations are achieved. The body responds rather elegantly to situations that threaten or deplete its supply of fuel. With no carbohydrates, the muscles are forced to become more effective at using fat for energy. Following a long run, more glycogen is synthesized and stored than what was previously present, thus increasing endurance. The more the glycogen tank is emptied, the faster it's refilled. The extra glycogen packed into the muscles increases a runner's ability to hold his marathon pace to the finish. To create the largest muscle glycogen storage possible, runners need to deplete muscle glycogen on a regular basis.

Since ingesting carbohydrates during long runs provides muscles with an accessible fuel, the three adaptations runners want to achieve—the muscles' reliance on fat, the liver's ability to make new glucose, and the depletion and subsequent resynthesis of more glycogen—are blunted. Therefore, to maximize physiological adaptations and improve marathon performance, runners should go without ingesting carbohydrates on long runs.

The marathon itself, however, is another story. In the marathon, it's important to maintain blood glucose levels for as long as possible to maintain the pace. Research has shown that supplementation with carbohydrate during prolonged exercise delays fatigue. Runners should begin ingesting glucose about 30 minutes before they start to feel fatigued so the glucose has time to be absorbed into the blood, where it can be used for energy. They can continue ingesting glucose every 20 minutes to maintain blood glucose levels. While the strategy is different for the marathon compared to training, runners don't ever want to do something in the marathon that they haven't done in training. Specifically, they don't want to consume carbohydrates in the marathon when they have never done so during long training runs; otherwise, they may end up with some gastrointestinal distress in the race. Therefore, they need to balance the physiological purpose of the long runs with the practical gastrointestinal issue of consuming carbohydrates while running. To attend to both issues, runners should alternate long runs, during which they consume and don't consume carbohydrates.

#23: Train to strengths.

While improving weakness will make runners more successful, focusing on strengths will ultimately lead to the best result. Therefore, training should always be skewed in favor of what runners are naturally good at. It's best to target weaknesses in the preseason or early season phases of training and focus on strengths later in the season, as runners get closer to the most important races.

Endurance-type runners should focus on more aerobic work (mileage and acidosis threshold workouts). Speed-type runners can get by on less aerobic work (but still adequate enough to meet the demands of the race) and emphasize interval training. Since many runners train to race the same distance, runners with different strengths can follow different paths to meet at the same point. For example, an endurance-type runner should initially do longer intervals, trying to get faster with training, such as 1,200-meter repetitions at 5K race pace, increasing speed to 3K race pace or decreasing the recovery as training progresses. The speed-type runner should do shorter intervals, trying to hold the pace for longer with training, such as 800-meter repetitions at 3K race pace, increasing the distance to 1,200 meters or increasing the number of repetitions as training progresses.

#24: Get a bigger heart.

The amount of blood the heart pumps with each contraction of its left ventricle (the heart's largest chamber that is responsible for sending blood to every part of the body except the lungs) is called the stroke volume. Multiplying the stroke volume by the heart rate results in the amount of blood pumped by the heart each minute, called the cardiac output. The larger the left ventricle, the more blood it can hold; the more blood it can hold, the more blood it can pump. Interval training gives the cardiovascular system a very heavy load to deal with, because of the repeated attainment of the heart's maximum stroke volume and cardiac output.

From an evolutionary perspective, an organism's structural design evolves to cope with the stresses to which it is subjected, which has led to the theory that an organism's structural design is regulated by its functional demand. As preeminent anatomist Ewald Weibel wrote, "the quantity of structure incorporated into an animal's functional system is matched to what is needed: enough but not too much." While the body's structural form has developed from millions of years of evolution, structural changes can also occur in the short term in response to training. With the right stimuli, bones increase their density, muscle fibers increase their metabolic machinery, and cardiac muscle grows larger. If structure and function are matched to the demand, it's logical to assume that if the demand is increased, the amount of change that takes place will ultimately increase to keep pace with the increased demand—and that's exactly what happens. Imagine what the heart goes through during training. After a difficult workout, the heart says, "This person is running hard workouts on a regular basis that cause me to reach my maximum capability to pump blood. If he keeps doing this and I don't do something, I'm not going to be able to survive." Thus, in response to the imposed threat of running at the heart's maximum ability to pump blood, the heart responds by increasing its contractility (pumping strength) and by enlarging its most important chamber (called left ventricular hypertrophy) so that more blood and oxygen can be sent to the working skeletal muscles. Pretty elegant. So characteristic is a large heart of genetically gifted and highly trained runners that it is considered a physiological condition by the scientific and medical communities called "athlete's heart."

While most runners may never attain the heart size and associated cardiac output of an Olympic champion, specific training can make the heart larger and increase its stroke volume and cardiac output. To cause left ventricular hypertrophy and achieve athlete's heart, athletes should run intervals that bring them to within a few beats of their maximum heart rate by the end of each work period. This speed corresponds to close to one-mile race pace for recreational runners and close to two-mile race pace (10 to 15 seconds per mile faster than 5K race pace) for trained runners. The work periods should last three to five minutes, and the time of the recovery intervals, during which runners should continue jogging to keep heart rate elevated, should be equal to or slightly less than the work periods.

#25: Live at altitude, but train at sea level.

Since many of the world's best runners live at altitude, namely the Kenyans and Ethiopians, quite a lot of attention has been given to altitude training as a way to improve distance running performance. While altitude may not be the reason for their success, altitude training may have some benefit if it is used correctly, just as other forms of training can have some benefit if they are used correctly. Living and running at altitude stimulates the production of red blood cells (called erythropoiesis, after erythropoietin, the hormone that stimulates their production) as part of acclimatization to compensate for the decreased oxygen, giving blood a greater oxygen-carrying capability when runners return to sea level. However, acclimatization to altitude does not completely counteract its fundamental stress. Changes in the cardiovascular system do not return to what is characteristic at sea level, preventing athletes from doing aerobic workouts at the same speed. Since VO_2max is lower at altitude, running at the same speed as at sea level will feel harder because runners are working at a higher percentage of (altitude) VO_2max. So, altitude training is a balancing act: making more red blood cells on the one hand versus training at slower speeds on the other hand. The trick is to not let the latter outweigh the former.

The slower speeds associated with altitude training has led to an interesting area of research that suggests that, to acquire the benefit of both worlds, it is better for endurance athletes to live at altitude to stimulate the production of red blood cells, but train at sea level to maintain a greater training intensity, a strategy called "live high/train low." Some studies have examined this issue by actually having athletes travel back and forth between altitude and sea level, while other studies have simulated altitude conditions by having athletes at sea level breathe different concentrations of oxygen for varying amounts of time during the day. There is some evidence that this live high/train low strategy may improve sea level performance by inducing the erythropoiesis associated with altitude exposure while maintaining sea-level training intensities. However, research has also shown that not all runners respond to altitude training to the same extent, with responders showing a greater concentration of erythropoietin in the blood and a smaller decrement in training speed at altitude than non-responders. Interestingly, research has shown that individuals who are very aerobically fit and have a high VO_2max at sea level experience a greater reduction in VO_2max at altitude compared to less fit individuals because fitter people exhibit a greater decrease in blood oxygen saturation at altitude. It seems that the more runners have to begin with, the more they have to lose. Thus, while altitude training may work for some runners, others would be better served by remaining at sea level where they can train at a faster pace.

For most runners, living at altitude and training at sea level is not practical. There are few places where runners can easily drive back and forth between the two. If runners want to try altitude training, another option is to train at altitude for a relatively short period of time so they can achieve the red blood cell production but not lose speed. The ideal altitude is 6,500 to 8,000 feet for at least four weeks to obtain the greatest erythropoietic benefit while minimizing the occurrence of acute mountain sickness (a condition caused by exposure to moderate to extreme altitudes characterized by headaches, nausea, loss of appetite, and lethargy). To maintain sea-level training intensity while at altitude, athletes should run "sea-level speed" workouts in addition to altitude workouts. They should run at the same pace as they would run at sea level but cut the length of the work periods so they can run at sea-level speed. For example, a runner who normally runs 1,000-meter repeats at sea level in 3:45 (6:00 pace) might try running 600-meter repeats at altitude in 2:15 (6:00 pace).

#26: Train consistently.

The number-one secret of training is that there are no secrets. It takes a lot of consistent work, over a long period of time, to meet running potential. That's because many of the adaptations to training result from the expression of genes and the formation of new proteins, which is a slow process. If runners miss workouts, it will take much longer to get where they want to go, if they get there at all. Consistent training leads to results. If runners want to be successful, the consistency of weekly mileage and other workouts is just as important as the mileage and workouts themselves. Whether running for fitness and weight loss or training for the Olympics, training loses its value if it has constant interruptions. Runners who've ever been injured and have been forced to take time off from running know how quickly fitness is lost. With consistent training, a constant need for adaptation is introduced. If the training stimulus is removed, not only are there no further adaptations, there is also no longer any reason to keep the adaptations that have occurred. So the body gets rid of them. It will take runners much longer to see results if they run two days this week, four days next week, three days the week after, six days the week after that, two days the following week, and so forth. If athletes really want to see results and run winning races, they must be consistent with applying the training stress—week after week, month after month, year after year.

#27: Train with a purpose.

Most runners train haphazardly, without any real sense of purpose, and then are often disappointed with their racing results. When training with a purpose and understanding the reason for every workout, runners can train more precisely and set themselves up for success. Runners should understand the purpose for every day of training, and then design a workout to meet the purpose. If the runner has a coach, he should ask the coach to explain the purpose of the workouts so he can become a part of the process.

Meeting the purpose of a workout is often problematic when runners of different abilities train in a group or as part of a team. During an interval workout, for example, the faster runners get a lot of recovery relative to the work periods, as they wait for the slower runners to finish. The slower runners always run too fast in an attempt to keep up with the faster runners, and get less time for recovery before the start of the next work period. There may be a few runners in the middle of the pack who get the optimal stimulus. In a team dynamic, unless the coach takes strict care to design the workout for each runner, using the right pace, the right duration of the work periods, and the right amount of recovery, few of the runners get an optimal workout that specifically meets the intended purpose.

For all workouts, whether they are easy runs, acidosis threshold workouts, $\dot{V}O_2$max intervals, or anaerobic capacity intervals, athletes should run as slow as possible while still obtaining the desired result since the goal of training is to obtain the greatest benefit while incurring the least amount of stress. Of all the workouts runners do, the easy runs, which comprise the bulk of their training, are least tied to a specific pace because the volume of work done is more important than the speed at which it's done. Many of the physiological and biochemical adaptations that runners are trying to obtain are volume-dependent, not intensity-dependent. However, they don't want to run so slow that they don't provide a stimulus for adaptation. Easy runs should be done at about one-and-a-half to two minutes per mile slower than current 5K race pace. As runners increase their weekly mileage, they may need to run slower to accommodate the extra volume, which can be fatiguing in itself. If using a heart rate monitor, runners can aim for 70 to 75 percent of maximum heart rate, although heart rate may fluctuate depending on hills, weather, and terrain. The single biggest mistake competitive runners make is running too fast on their easy days. By doing so, they add unnecessary stress to their legs without any extra benefit and they won't be able to run as much quality on harder days. Speed-type runners (runners who fare better at shorter races) will have a greater difference between their race pace and easy running pace compared to endurance-type runners (runners who fare better at longer races). Slowing down the easy runs has at least three benefits: it decreases the chance of injury, it allows runners to get more out of their harder days because there will be less residual fatigue, and it allows them to increase their overall weekly mileage.

Acidosis threshold workouts are the most difficult type for runners to run at the correct speed since it requires holding back and not pushing the pace. There's a comfortably hard feeling to the pace that requires practice. However, if runners understand the purpose of each workout, whether it's an acidosis threshold workout or something else, it's easier to run at the right pace because they understand what they're trying to accomplish.

#28: Use benchmarks.

A benchmark can help runners determine fitness level and allow them to test whether they are on track with their progress. Whether they use a time trial, a specific workout, or a race, runners should include benchmarks in their training every couple of months. Following are some good benchmarks for different races. From these benchmarks, runners can predict with a good degree of accuracy what time they should be able to run in an upcoming race.

Mile	**5K**	**10K**	**Marathon**
• 8 to 10 x 400 meters at mile race pace with a 1:1 work:rest ratio • 2 sets of 400/800/400 meters at mile race pace with 1:00 recovery and 5:00 recovery between sets	• 2-mile time trial • 3,000-meter/ 2-mile race	• 6 x 1 mile at 10K pace with 2:00 recovery • 5K race	• 7- to 10-mile tempo run at 10-15 seconds per mile slower than acidosis threshold pace • 16-mile run, with second half at marathon pace • Half-marathon race

2

Winning Pre-Racing Strategies

#29: Know the opponent's strengths and weaknesses, and capitalize on them.

Knowing the opponent's strengths and weakness can help athletes design a race plan that will help them beat opponents. For example, if an athlete wants to beat a specific opponent, he should know whether the opponent tends to go out too fast when the race starts, which parts of the race the opponent is weaker, and whether the opponent has a good finishing kick. For example, if a runner knows that John always goes out too fast and gets slower with each successive mile, the runner can feel confident that if he lets John go in the beginning and stays relatively close, he'll pass him late in the race when he fatigues. If the runner knows Jane has a better kick than she does, she needs to be far enough ahead of her in the latter stages of the race so that any kick that Jane uses will be too late to catch her. Conversely, if the runner knows she has a better kick than Jane, she needs to stay within striking distance of her until the final stages of the race so that she can use her kick to her advantage. A runner could have the best finishing speed of anyone in the race, but if he is 20 seconds behind his opponent with a quarter mile to go, his kick is not going to do any good. The timing of the kick is also important. Many times a kick is started either too early or too late. Runners have to know how far out from the finish line they can sustain a kick.

#30: Hydrate.

Water is vital for many chemical reactions that occur inside body cells, including the production of energy for muscle contraction. Since water is the major component of the body, when water is lost, there are consequences. A major consequence of dehydration is an increase in core body temperature while running, with body temperature rising 0.15 to 0.2 degrees Celsius for every one percent of body weight lost due to sweating. Running performance declines with only a 2 to 3 percent loss of body weight due to fluid loss.

On a hot day, body temperature, already on the rise from muscle contraction, increases even more. Since the primary mechanism for cooling the body is through the evaporation of sweat from the skin's surface, sweat rate increases. As a result, body water is lost, and the runner will begin to become dehydrated.

Since the effects of heat and dehydration on physiological function combine to have an even greater effect than either one alone, being dehydrated when running in the heat causes running performance to decline even more, and can even be a recipe for disaster, with the risk of heat-related illnesses rising dramatically. The problem is that running in the heat makes it very difficult to prevent dehydration, since sweat rate exceeds the ability to ingest and absorb fluid while running. While low- to moderate-intensity running typically results in sweat losses of 0.8 to 1.4 liters per hour, high environmental temperature combined with high-intensity running can increase sweat rate to 1.4 to 2 liters per hour. However, the gastrointestinal system can absorb only about 0.8 to 1.2 liters of fluid per hour. Thus, heat stress and dehydration often occur together.

Accompanying the increase in thermal strain when exercising in the heat is a greater cardiovascular strain. Profuse sweating to increase evaporative cooling causes a loss of plasma volume from the blood, and total blood volume decreases. When blood volume decreases, stroke volume (the volume of blood pumped by the heart with each beat) decreases. A decreased stroke volume means oxygen flow to the muscles is then compromised, and an athlete's running pace slows. To compensate for the decreased stroke volume, the heart must work harder to pump blood and heart rate drifts upward in an attempt to maintain cardiac output (the volume of blood pumped by the heart each minute) and blood pressure. Heart rate increases three to five beats per minute for every one percent of body weight loss from dehydration.

Because of the decrease in exercise performance and the potential health danger of dehydration, plenty of research has been done (and an onslaught of sports drinks has been marketed) on strategies to overcome, or at least blunt, the effects of dehydration. Beginning the workout or race fully hydrated or even "hyperhydrating" beforehand can delay dehydration during the run, maintain running performance, and decrease the risk for heat-related illnesses. Pre-race fluid intake enhances the ability to control body temperature and increases plasma volume to maintain cardiac output. Runners should drink before they run in the heat so they begin every workout fully hydrated, and continue to drink during workouts and races longer than one hour.

The best hydration fluids are those that contain sodium, which stimulates the kidneys to retain water. However, if the run is of a low intensity and lasts less than an hour, water alone is sufficient. A good indicator of hydration level is the color of urine. The lighter the urine color, the better the level of hydration. Urine should look like lemonade rather than apple juice.

Optimal Hydration Strategies

- Drink 16 ounces (480 milliliters) two hours before the race.
- Drink about 8 ounces (240 milliliters) every 15 to 20 minutes during long races. Runners who sweat heavily should drink more.
- After the race, drink 15 ounces per pound of body weight (1 liter/kilogram) lost during the race.
- Consume 0.5 to 0.7 gram of sodium (about one-tenth of a teaspoon of salt) per liter of fluid before, during, and after the race (this is necessary only if the race lasts more than 60 minutes or if the runner has a sodium deficiency).

Glycerol

Drinks that contain glycerol (the structural backbone of triglycerides) create an osmotic gradient in the circulation that causes fluid retention, which facilitates hyperhydration, protects against dehydration, and maintains core body temperature.

- Consume 1.2 grams per kilogram of body weight in a 20 percent glycerol solution within 30 minutes, followed by 26 milliliters of water per kilogram of body weight distributed over 90 minutes before the run.
- Consume 0.125 gram per kilogram of body weight mixed in 5 milliliters of fluid per kilogram of body weight during the run.
- Consume 1.0 gram per kilogram of body weight mixed in 1.5 liters of fluid after the run.

#31: Play head games with opponents.

Psychology is a big part of racing. Oftentimes, an athlete can get into the other runners' heads before the race even begins. A well-placed word to another runner, acting very confident, even throwing an intimidating look at another runner can all go a long way to getting inside opponents' heads and breaking their confidence. Sometimes, that's all that is needed to beat an opponent. Words and body language can be powerful tools. For example, a runner can say to his opponent, "I'm feeling great today. I'm going to run a personal best." And then carry himself with a lot of confidence. Even if a runner is not feeling great or likely to run a personal best, what matters is that the opponent thinks that's the case.

#32: Visualize the race before it happens.

I know an Olympic 400-meter runner who sat in his dark dorm room closet in the Olympic Village the night before his race so he could visualize it. Since he didn't know what lane on the track he would be assigned until shortly before the race, he visualized running the 400-meter race from each lane on the track, seeing himself run each curve, each straightaway, each of the other runners. He visualized the crowd and the cameras. The next day, he won the gold medal and set a new world record.

The mind is a powerful tool. Visualizing the race before running it allows the runner to experience it beforehand, making the experience familiar and thus making him less nervous. If the experience is familiar, the runner will feel more comfortable. The athlete should practice visualizing the race each day for a few days before it, seeing the whole experience. He should try to use all of his senses in the visualization—seeing the track or race course, feeling the contraction of the muscles as the legs push forcefully against the ground, feeling the arms pumping and driving him forward, seeing himself blowing past his opponents, hearing his feet touch the ground, smelling the air, seeing himself react to other runners' moves, feeling his pace, and tasting the experience. Then, when it's time for the race, he will have already run it. The runner can visualize from an internal perspective, seeing the race through his own eyes as he runs it, or from an external perspective, as a spectator observing himself run the race. Either way, visualizing the result an athlete wants to see as many times as possible ingrains that result into the mind.

#33: Know what pace can be sustained in the race.

When racing, athletes don't run at some arbitrary intensity. The percentages of specific physiological variables, such as $\dot{V}O_2$max and acidosis threshold, that an athlete can sustain for a specific amount of time are predictable. For example, the longer the race, the lower the percent $\dot{V}O_2$max at which he'll run it. The speed at $\dot{V}O_2$max can be sustained for only about 7 to 10 minutes. Talented, highly-trained runners race 3,000 meters or two miles at 100 percent $\dot{V}O_2$max, 5,000 meters at 90 to 95 percent $\dot{V}O_2$max, and a marathon at 80 to 85 percent $\dot{V}O_2$max. Workouts are invaluable for providing knowledge of fitness level and for predicting an average race pace (assuming such things like the terrain and the weather are accounted for). Runners often ignore the workouts they have done when they get to a race, and start the race at a pace they cannot sustain the entire distance. Athletes should learn from their workouts and know going into the race what pace they can expect to sustain.

Using the following guidelines can help to predict a race pace from workouts. The pace differentials change with the difference in performance level (i.e., a faster runner can sustain a pace that is farther above his acidosis threshold compared to a slower runner because the race takes less time to complete).

- *5K Pace:* 10 to 15 seconds per mile faster than acidosis threshold (AT) workouts for recreational runners; 25 to 30 seconds per mile faster than AT workouts for highly trained runners; 10 to 15 seconds per mile slower than $\dot{V}O_2$max interval workouts for trained runners.
- *10K Pace:* Equal or very close to the pace of AT workouts for recreational runners (those slower than about 40 minutes for 10K); 10 to 15 seconds per mile faster than AT workouts for highly trained runners; 25 to 30 seconds per mile slower than $\dot{V}O_2$max interval workouts for trained runners.
- *Marathon Pace:* More than 60 seconds per mile slower than AT workouts for recreational runners; about 45 to 60 seconds per mile slower than AT workouts for good runners; about 20 seconds per mile slower than AT workouts for highly trained and elite runners.

#34: Consume caffeine before the race.

Given its well-recognized property as a central nervous system stimulant, most people consume caffeine to keep themselves awake and delay fatigue. A number of studies have found that ingesting caffeine can also improve running performance. Most research suggests that the maximum benefit of caffeine, which can make a run feel easier even though the athlete is running faster, is seen at a relatively small dose (2 to 3 milligrams per kilogram of body weight) ingested about an hour before a race. However, caffeine does not work for everyone. It seems to work better for people who are "caffeine-naive" (i.e., people who don't usually consume caffeine on a regular basis). Like any other ergogenic aid, caffeine is not without its side effects: nervousness, anxiety, sleeplessness, stomach aches, and diarrhea. Since individuals often respond differently to nutritional treatments, runners should practice using caffeine in training before trying it for a race.

#35: Give a self-pep talk before the race.

Everyone needs to be encouraged, motivated, and inspired. Sometimes, that encouragement, motivation, and inspiration can come from other people, but it can also come from within. After all, running is, at its essence, all about the runner. So he should give a self-pep talk before the race. The runner should remind himself of the hard work he has done and how he can use the race as an opportunity to learn about himself. He should ignite the fire within and pump himself up. He can look himself in the mirror if he wants, and tell himself to stand up to his hopes and fears and run the best race he can.

#36: Have specific, meaningful goals in mind for the race.

All successful people, whether they sell used cars or win an Olympic gold medal, have specific, definable, and difficult but attainable goals. Goals provide direction, motivation, and a sense of purpose. By having specific goals for races, it allows athletes to get away from thinking about the race as a whole, which can be overwhelming. It also allows for something positive to be taken from each race, even if the overall outcome is disappointing. For instance, if the athlete wants to pass at least one runner on every hill during the race, and succeed at doing so, he can at least be happy about accomplishing that, despite a disappointing race performance. A runner should have one or two goals for each race that are within his control, such as the following:

- I will start my kick with a quarter mile to go.
- I will run even splits for each mile or each lap.
- I will pass at least one runner on every hill.

It is important for a runner to say to himself, "I *will* do this," rather than, "I *want* to do this." A person may want to earn a million dollars, but the likelihood of that happening is not as good as if he says, "I *will* earn a million dollars" and mean it.

Having a specific goal for each race also allows a runner to work on parts of the race that need to be worked on so that when it is time for the most important race, he will have practiced all of the components of the race that he needs to practice and have all of the tools in his arsenal to run his best race.

#37: Have a race plan.

A race plan takes some of the unknowns out and gives athletes something to focus on besides the butterflies in their stomachs. Runners should break down the race into smaller segments, concentrating on each segment at a time. For the mile, it may mean breaking down the race into 200- or 400-meter segments; for a 5K, breaking it down into each mile; and for the marathon, breaking it down into each mile or each 5K. Runners should have a firm idea about how they want to run each of those segments. What pace do they want to run? What place do they want to be in?

#38: Go to the bathroom before the race.

Although the urge to go to the bathroom is often suppressed while running (especially during long races) to conserve water and prevent dehydration, nervousness and anxiety before the race often intensify that urge, so runners should take care of business before the race. The discomfort associated with racing also often causes gastrointestinal distress, which can become a major issue in the race. Runners should try to run a race on as empty a colon as possible.

#39: Get to the race with plenty of time to spare.

When I was in high school, my cross-country teammates and I would often walk the courses before our races to familiarize ourselves with them. Before our freshmen district championships, we were out walking the course when we discovered that we were a bit lost, and the race was going to start soon. Our coach came looking for us and brought us back to the starting line area, where we had to rush to get ready. I didn't have time to complete a warm-up or go to the bathroom or any pre-race rituals. I was so full of anxiety, my coach had to pin my race number to my uniform because I couldn't keep my hands still enough to maneuver the safety pins. I was the favorite to win the race, with one of my teammates, who had never beaten me, the favorite to place second, so I had some pressure on me. I got to the starting line just in time for the gun. The race started off well, with me and my teammate taking the early lead. We were running together for a while, but by the time I had gotten to the one-mile mark of the two-mile race, I could feel the anxiety in my stomach and my lunch in my colon. Without going into messy details, I ran the rest of that race, trying to hold back the strong urge to go to the bathroom. My teammate picked up the pace, and I couldn't go with him, too focused on the urge that was quickly starting to reveal itself. Somehow, I held on for second place, although I was very disappointed because I was expected to win. It was the first time my teammate had beaten me, and I knew that would give him confidence for the rest of the season. Immediately after the race, I ran to the bathroom, where I spent the next 15 minutes.

The last thing runners want before the race is to rush. Rushing can lead to excess anxiety, which does nothing to help an athlete run a winning race. Runners should get to the race as early as possible. They should account for such things as traffic, finding a parking spot, picking up their race number and T-shirt, warm-up, stretching, waiting lines for portable restrooms, and any other pre-race rituals.

#40: Get a scouting report of the opponents.

I used to coach a runner in her thirties who was going to run the 5,000 meters in an indoor track meet against college runners. Knowing one of the local college runners against whom she was going to compete, I approached her a few days before the race and asked her what time she was expecting to run. She had no idea why I was asking, probably thinking I was just making conversation. I knew two things about this runner—one was that she wasn't capable of running the time she told me and the other was that she, along with her college teammates, had a history of starting races much too fast and slowing down with each mile of the race. Knowing what time she was shooting for helped me to advise my athlete about how to run the race and gave her insider information about what to expect from her opponent. We developed a race strategy around that information. The strategy worked—as expected, the college runner went out much too fast and my athlete ran past her opponent in the latter stages of the race. Scouting the competition can help runners develop a winning racing strategy.

#41: When traveling to a race at altitude, start the race at a slower pace and arrive either at least two weeks before the race or as close as possible to the race.

The higher the elevation and the longer the race, the greater the decline in performance, so runners cannot expect to race at the same speed as at sea level. Starting the race at the same speed will only cause a greater amount of fatigue. Since the same aerobic pace at altitude will feel harder than at sea level due to the reduction in $\dot{V}O_2$max at altitude, the pace at altitude should be adjusted to make the race physiologically equivalent to a race at sea level. Unless a runner is able to train at altitude for at least two weeks before the race, he should arrive as close as possible to the race. The physiological changes that occur at altitude exhibit the greatest detrimental effect on performance between 10 and 14 days of exposure. Over the following few weeks, the body acclimatizes, such that the consequence of those changes are less severe.

#42: Warm up correctly before the race.

The warm-up serves two primary purposes: to prepare the runner for the physical demands of the race and to improve a muscle's dynamics so that it is less prone to injury. Specifically, the warm-up:

- Raises body temperature, which stimulates the dissociation of oxygen from hemoglobin, providing more oxygen to the working muscles
- Raises heart rate and causes vasodilation, which increases blood flow through the active tissues
- Increases the activity of enzymes involved in metabolism, resulting in a faster metabolic rate and a quicker regeneration of ATP for muscle contraction
- Causes sweating, which improves thermoregulation
- Reduces perceived exertion in the early parts of the race
- Increases the speed of nerve transmission, increasing the speed of muscle contraction
- Protects muscles from possible injury by requiring a greater length of stretch and force to be achieved to produce a tear

How long and how vigorously runners warm up depends on their level of conditioning, the length of the race, and the environmental temperature. In general, the higher the level of conditioning, the shorter the race, and the lower the environmental temperature, the longer and more vigorous the warm-up. The lower the level of conditioning, the less time will be needed to increase body temperature. A long, vigorous warm-up in a less fit runner will also add fatigue, which will be detrimental to race performance. The shorter the race, the faster the pace, so more time and greater intensity is needed to feel ready to run a fast pace from the start. Finally, the higher the environmental temperature, the easier it is to raise the body temperature and overheat, so the length of the warm-up should be decreased when it's hot and humid.

The warm-up should start slowly and get progressively faster until the pace matches the pace that the athlete will run in the race. The runner should be sweating mildly, but not fatigued. For races 10K and shorter, the athlete should run one to two miles very easy. Then, he should do two or three 30- to 60-second runs at acidosis threshold pace, followed by two or three 20- to 30-second runs at race pace. These short runs should be finished about five minutes before the race. Many runners will do short sprints while waiting at the start line, but that often puts them in a fast running mode, which causes them to go out too quickly when the gun goes off. If doing short sprints is the last thing done before the start of the race, the runner will be more likely to sprint when the gun goes off because he's put himself in that mode. For races longer than 10K (in particular half-marathon and marathon), it's not necessary (and may even be detrimental) to include much, if any, fast running as part of the warm-up since there is a need to conserve carbohydrates for the race, which get used when running fast.

#43: Protect oneself in the heat.

I grew up as a runner in New Jersey, where it can get downright sticky in the summertime, as stepping outside the air-conditioned house feels like walking into a steam room. In addition to wearing loose-fitting, moisture-wicking, light-colored clothes that reflect the sunlight, the two most important strategies for running a race in the heat are hydration and acclimatization.

Hydrate

Hydration was fully discussed in #30. Runners can delay dehydration, maintain their pace during a race, and decrease the risk for heat-related illnesses by beginning the race fully hydrated or even hyperhydrating before the race. Pre-race fluid intake enhances the ability to control body temperature and increases plasma volume to maintain cardiac output. Runners should drink fluids containing sodium before a race in the heat so they begin the race fully hydrated, and continue to drink during a race longer than one hour.

Acclimatize

Chronically exposing oneself to a hot and humid environment simulates adaptations that lesson the stress. Cardiovascular adaptations to running in the heat (e.g., decreased heart rate, increased plasma volume) are nearly complete within three to six days, while rectal temperature and electrolyte concentration changes take nine to 10 days. Full acclimatization is complete after two weeks, as the increased sweating response catches up to the other adaptations. Therefore, runners should take two weeks of slowly introducing themselves to the heat to be fully acclimatized and prepared for the race, especially if it's a long race. While racing in the heat will always present a stress, acclimatization has a moderate prophylactic effect, minimizing the stress and reducing the risk of heat-related illnesses.

#44: Control nerves at the starting line.

Every runner gets nervous before a race. That's perfectly normal. Being nervous means that the runner cares about the outcome of the race. The important thing for runners is to not let nervousness get the better of them and prevent them from running a winning race. They should acknowledge that nervousness, but use it as fuel. A few things can be done to minimize nervousness at the starting line.

Routine

There's familiarity in routine. Runners should come up with pre-race routines that include warm-up, stretching, bathroom, visualization, putting on racing shoes, and anything else they might do before a race, leading right up to the starting line. Everything should be done in the same order for every race.

Breathe

Runners should take a few deep breaths at the starting line to center themselves, sharpen their focus, and block out everything else.

Positive Self-Talk

Runners should remind themselves of all the work they've done to get to the starting line and that they're ready for a great performance. They should try repeating a positive sentence or phrase, like "I can do this!" or "I am ready for a great performance!"

#45: Say something debilitating to an opponent at the starting line.

More talent, smarter training, and superior fitness aside, a number of tricks can be used to gain an advantage over another runner. One of those tricks is what is said to an opponent and how it is said. Since races never have any downtime, the only time runners have to verbally communicate with one another is at the starting line (unless they're running side-by-side with someone during the race). The starting line can be a great time to get inside an opponent's head and make him doubt himself. When a runner is waiting for the race to start, he can say to his opponent, "You haven't been running well lately. What's wrong?" A comment like this can have a debilitating effect on an opponent's confidence, which will likely affect his race. Even if he has been running well lately, the comment will make him think otherwise and take him out of his game. To attempt to answer the question, he'll try to come up with something that's wrong, to explain why he has apparently not been running well. The power of suggestion goes a long way.

While racing is very physical, runners should not underestimate the very important mental side, so they should do something to get in their opponent's head and break his confidence.

#46: Dress for success.

This strategy is probably a familiar one, although not in context with running a race. How runners appear when they show up to the starting line is just as important and has the same effect as what they look like when going to a business meeting or on a date. People get only one chance to make a first impression. If a runner shows up to the starting line dressed in a torn cotton T-shirt and basketball shorts that come down to his knees, no one will take him seriously. Showing up to the starting line in a singlet and racing shorts and shoes, other runners will notice and know that this runner means business. They will have a great amount of respect for him. By taking the time to dress like a winner, an athlete will be that much closer to running like one. Dressing sharp makes runners feel faster, and if they feel faster, they'll run faster.

#47: Don't run a race on an empty stomach.

While many races are run early in the morning, athletes should not run a race on an empty stomach. Racing, regardless of the distance, requires carbohydrates for energy. When people first awake in the morning, blood glucose and muscle and liver glycogen are low since it has been many hours since their last meal. Even if the race is in the afternoon, blood glucose may be low if it has been a few hours since the runner last ate. When glucose is unavailable, muscles are forced to rely on fat, which slows down the pace since it takes longer to regenerate ATP for muscle contraction when using fat compared to when using carbohydrates. Runners need to have glucose ready to use in their blood so they can run a faster pace.

The pre-race meal, which restocks the liver with glycogen and elevates blood sugar, improves energy level prior to the start of the race. Runners should aim for 300 to 400 calories of carbohydrates and protein, eating food that is easily digestible, such as toast, bananas, scrambled eggs, rice- or corn-based cereal, pasta, and potato. They should stay away from fiber, especially if they're running a long race, as fiber can wreak havoc on the gastrointestinal system.

#48: Sleep.

This strategy is obvious. Runners need adequate sleep to perform at their best. Since all of the adaptations to training occur during recovery from training rather than during the training itself, sleep is very important for sufficient recovery. Sleep is an individual matter. Runners should experiment with the number of hours of sleep to determine what is adequate for them. For a few days leading up to the race, runners should make sure to get at least that amount every night so that they feel refreshed.

3

Winning During-Racing Strategies

#49: Run even or negative splits.

I used to coach a talented runner who ran the first mile of every race too fast, only to slow down dramatically during the latter segments and end up disappointed with the result. He thought he was better than his workouts, and he let his competitive spirit and pre-race adrenaline obscure his knowledge of his true fitness level. It was frustrating to watch him start off so well and get slower with each successive lap of the track. It was only after he understood proper pacing that he saw the level of success we both knew he could attain.

The single biggest mistake runners make when they race is that they start out too fast, way above their fitness level. They either ignore or do not learn from their training what pace is realistically sustainable for the entire race. The faster athletes run the first half of a race, the more their muscles rely on oxygen-independent (anaerobic) metabolism to generate energy. With the greater reliance on oxygen-independent metabolism and muscular work comes an increase in muscle and blood acidosis and the accumulation of metabolites that cause fatigue. Whether the race is a mile or a marathon, runners can't put running time in the bank. They will end up losing more time in the end than what they gained by being ahead of schedule in the beginning. No matter how strong a runner's will is, the metabolic condition caused by running too fast too early will force him to slow down during subsequent stages of the race.

The best way to run the fastest possible race and beat others is by running the second half of the race at a pace that is equal to or slightly faster than the first half (even or negative splits). To negative split a race, a runner must have accurate knowledge of his fitness level, confidence to stick to the plan when others have taken the early pace out too fast, and a good dose of self-restraint. The most economical racing strategy, when wanting to achieve a specific time rather than a specific place, is to prevent large fluctuations in pace and run as evenly as possible to keep muscle acidosis as low as possible until nearing the finish. When running a race, runners should ask themselves within the first mile (or the first lap or two of a track race), "Can I really hold this pace the entire way?" They must be honest with themselves. If the answer is yes, then they should go for it. If the answer is no, then they should back off the pace so they can have a better race. The best races come when runners are in control of the race the whole time and able to run faster in the closing stages, rather than when the race is controlling them and they're just hanging on to the pace, waiting for the finish line to come. Remember, they don't give out medals for crossing the race's halfway mark first. They give out medals only at the finish line, which is at the finish of the race.

If there is one winning racing strategy that will enable athletes to run a better, faster race on that day (disregarding for the moment the training that led up to it), whether it is a mile or a marathon, running even or slightly negative splits is it.

#50: Sit and kick.

Let other runners set the pace in a race. It takes more energy to run from the front than it does to sit behind others. So runners should let their competitors do the early work. Sitting right off the competitors' shoulders or right behind them and staring at their backs, runners can let the competition pull them along. Then, at some predetermined distance from the finish line, runners can make a strong, decisive move and surge past the competition. Runners can often catch them off-guard, and they won't be able to respond. If the opponent has a strong kick, runners can make their move early and try to put as much distance as possible between them so that by the time the competitor begins to kick, they're too far ahead to be caught.

#51: Surge.

Surging involves picking up the pace during a run or race. A change of pace in a race, even when it's a change to a faster pace, can often make runners feel more comfortable and give them a boost of confidence. A mid-race surge is also a great way to separate from other runners, especially those who have a stronger finishing kick. Good times for runners to surge are when wanting to break away from opponents, at the top of a hill, and when sensing that the runner next to them is laboring.

Runners should practice running surges in workouts so they can execute them in a race. During a run, runners should pick up the pace for 20 to 30 seconds, with the surge starting abruptly and ending gradually. If running on a team or with a group of people, surging can also be practiced with a group. The group or team should break into small groups of runners of similar abilities. Each group runs together for 4 to 5 miles, with one runner being designated as the pacesetter, whose job it is to surge at different points in the run. When the pacesetter surges, the other runners practice reacting to the surge and picking up the pace to match the pacesetter. Each runner in the group can also surge whenever he wants to, with the other runners reacting to the surge and covering the move instead of having just one pacesetter.

#52: Stay close to an opponent at all times.

If a large gap opens up between runners and their opponents, it can be very difficult to close the gap and beat them. Runners must try to do whatever they can to remain close to an opponent at all times during the race. If the opponent does get ahead, runners should know how much rope they can give the opponent that is still safe for them to make up the distance before the finish line and be sure not to give any more rope than that.

#53: Run fast up a hill.

Many runners slow down in anticipation of and while running a hill. Attacking a hill is a great chance to pull away from other runners in a race. To practice running hills, runners can try these workouts:

- Run 5 to 6 x 1/2-mile uphill (5 to 8 percent incline) at 5K race pace effort with a jog back down as recovery.
- Sprint 8 to 10 x 100 meters uphill (15 to 20 percent incline) with a jog back down as recovery.
- Run 4 to 8 x 200 to 400 meters uphill, running the bottom of the hill at race pace effort and accelerating the last 50 meters of the hill and 100 meters after cresting the top, with a jog back down as recovery.

When running hills, runners should exaggerate their arm swing, lean into the hill, and focus on pushing off with the ball of the foot.

#54: Run the first half to two thirds of the race with the head and the last third to half with the heart.

It's easy to be emotional at the start of a race, but running with emotions in the beginning rarely works. It often makes runners start out too fast, only to slow down during latter stages of the race when fatigue gets the better of them. The best runners usually go out too fast, but everyone goes with them, so when the best runner fades, all the others fade more and the best runner believes that going out fast is the way to run because it led to victory. The day that one of those other runners who is not as good as the best one runs a smart race, then the best runner no longer wins. Emotions and heart have a time and a place, but it's not in the first mile. To run a great race, an athlete must run at least the first half with his head, knowing what pace he can honestly sustain the entire way. It's better to pass 15 people in the middle of the race and get outkicked by three at the end than to look great outkicking three at the end but not pass anyone in the middle of the race. By running with their heads for the first half to two thirds of the race, runners can beat all the runners in the race who are not as fast as them, all the runners in the race who are of equal performance level, and half the runners in the race who are better than them. When it gets late in the race and a smart pace has been run from the beginning, that's the time for a runner to dig deep, let his emotions come to the forefront, run with his whole heart, and become the runner and the person he wants to be.

#55: Box in the opponent.

Runners can use other runners in the race or they can work together with other runners on their team to box in an opponent so he can't beat them. This strategy works especially well on the track. At the elite level, the Kenyans and Ethiopians have become well known for their team tactics, running from the front and blocking other runners from passing them. Forcing opponents into a box will not only make it harder for them to pass, it will frustrate them, which can make them panic and cause them to make strategic mistakes.

#56: Dictate the pace.

It's often easy to fall into other runners' race plans and let them control the race. But when dictating the pace, rather than an opponent doing so, it allows the race to play into the runner's hands. Pace may be dictated in many ways, including running the race from the front and making the pace slow to take advantage of a superior finishing kick compared to that of opponents, taking the pace out quickly or putting on a mid-race surge to pull away from the faster-finishing opponents, and changing the pace multiple times during the race with surges to beat a friend or rival.

#57: Learn to react to opponents' moves.

Races don't always go as planned. Sometimes, it's hard to predict what other runners will do and when they'll do it. Some runners will make their move early in the race to break it open, some runners will use a long, sustained surge far out from the finish line, and some runners will wait until very close to the end of the race, allowing other runners to do the work for as long as possible, then sprint past them before the finish line. Runners need to learn to react to when other runners make moves. Sometimes, cues can be picked up on from other runners that will indicate what they are about to do. For example, some runners may have a specific gesture or body movement they make right before they make a move. By being alert, runners can pick up on these movements.

To practice reacting to other runners' moves, it's helpful to run in a group of runners with similar abilities. Like the surge practice discussed in #51, runners can run together for 4 to 5 miles, with one runner being designated as the pacesetter, whose job it is to surge at different points in the run. When the pacesetter surges, runners can practice reacting to the surge and picking up the pace to match the pacesetter. The group can also have multiple pacesetters, each pacesetter surging whenever he wants to, with the other runners reacting to the surge and covering the move.

#58: Be aggressive.

Running is not a sport for timid people. To be successful, runners have to be aggressive at times in a race. Not aggressive to the point of pushing other runners to the side, but aggressive to the point of being assertive and running the race that they want to run. Sometimes, runners have to take control of the race and the other runners. Sometimes, runners have to take control of their own emotions. Being aggressive is especially important when racing on an indoor track, where runners can easily get bumped and pushed and spiked and forced to run the race from an outside lane. If a runner is aggressive, he can get out fast and claim a position on the inside.

#59: Engage in self-talk.

Believe it or not, successful people talk to themselves. Often, they have ongoing conversations with themselves, verbalizing and solidifying in their own heads what they want to accomplish. While a person may not want to talk to himself out loud in public for fear of being thought of as crazy, self-talk can be a very powerful strategy to run a successful race.

Unlike the 100-meter dash, which is over in a few seconds, distance races provide a lot of time to think. They are also physically uncomfortable, which can lead to negative thoughts and doubts about being able to hold the pace or beat other runners. Any time a negative thought enters their heads before or during a race, runners should say, "Stop" and replace it with a positive thought ("I'm strong," or "I'm fast," or "The other runners are even more fatigued than I am."). Early in the race, runners can say things to themselves to keep calm and relaxed. In the middle of the race, when starting to feel fatigued, runners can say things to keep encouraged to hold the pace. They may want to focus on a specific landmark on a road or cross-country course or lap of the track, and say to themselves, "Just hold the pace until I get to the landmark," or "Just hold the pace for one more lap." If runners hope to beat a specific runner, they can say to themselves, "Just stay with him for one more mile (or one more lap)." Toward the end of the race, they can say things to get fired up to run as fast as possible ("Go, go, go!"). Runners may even want to have a specific mantra for races, something that means a lot and triggers a feeling of empowerment.

#60: With one quarter to one half of a mile to go, be in the desired finishing place.

If runners want to win a race or have a goal to finish in a certain place or beat a certain opponent, they should do whatever they can to put themselves in the place they want to finish before the final sprint to the finish line (usually within a quarter- to a half-mile to go). This strategy puts the pressure on the opponent. Rather than having to catch the other runners before the finish line, athletes should make the other runners come from behind to beat them.

#61: Establish a rhythm early in the race.

Runners should use the early stages of the race to establish a rhythm. They should focus on their legs and breathing, trying to get as comfortable with the pace as possible. They can even try to get a beat in their head that they can follow. The earlier in the race that runners can establish a rhythm, the easier it will be to change gears later in the race.

#62: Focus and execute.

One of the keys to running a winning race is to focus on the task at hand and execute a race plan. It's often easy to let other things or outside or self-imposed pressures become distractions or allow the mind to wander during a race, but not allowing those things to become distractions, not allowing the mind to wander, and instead focusing on the performance to the exclusion of everything else will enable runners to perform at their highest level.

Just as with other aspects of a runner's performance, focusing takes practice. In training, runners should practice staying in the moment, not thinking about the next lap or the next mile. They should focus on staying connected to the task, to their body's movements. They should feel each leg push off the ground and forcefully drive them forward. Runners must practice increasing the length of time they focus, especially when training for a long race like a half-marathon or marathon. They can even make a game of it, challenging themselves to see how long they can focus on a task. Runners might choose a word or a movement to focus on that will act as a cue to sharpen their focus. If something happens during a workout or race that distracts them (and it often happens), runners should recognize that distraction and then immediately dismiss it so they can get back on track with their workout or race.

Once runners practice and learn how to focus on a task for the entire duration of the task, they are then free to execute their race plan, without fear or worry or anxiety about the result. They become the performance.

#63: Wear as little clothing as needed.

When racing, runners should wear as little clothing as needed and wear lightweight racing shoes. Any extra weight worsens running economy, as runners will consume more oxygen to transport the extra weight. Runners want to be as light as possible when they race.

#64: Run the shortest path.

When racing, runners should always run the shortest possible distance between two points. Courses are measured as the shortest distance between the start and finish lines. If an athlete runs wide, or doesn't follow the straight line between one part of the course and the other, he'll be running extra distance and his 5K may turn into a 5.1K. In close races, in which every second counts, runners may be able to beat an opponent by running tighter turns and being aware of the way the course is laid out so they can run the shortest path. If racing on the track, runners should not run the turns in lanes 2 or 3, instead positioning themselves in lane 1 without getting boxed in. If a runner does get boxed in on a turn, he should use the straightaway to get himself out of the box. (The only time when runners may have to run wide on a turn is the last turn on the last lap of the race, as they don't want to be boxed in that late in the race.) The longer the race, the more important running the shortest path becomes, as runners don't want a 26.2-mile marathon to turn into 26.6 miles!

#65: Draft.

Anyone who has run a race on a windy day has experienced how difficult it is to run into a headwind. The oxygen cost of running (and therefore the perception of effort) increases when running into a headwind, specifically as the square of the wind speed. The oxygen cost of running also increases as running speed increases. For example, when running a mile race at 4:28 pace (67 seconds per lap), about eight percent of the runner's energy is used to overcome air resistance. By drafting behind another runner, the runner can save about 80 percent of that energy, which is equivalent to about four seconds per lap. When running fast into a headwind, the oxygen cost increases dramatically. When running a race at six-minute mile pace, a headwind of 10 miles per hour is created. If running into a headwind of 10 miles per hour, that six-minute mile pace can feel closer to five-minute mile pace. By drafting behind another runner, runners can significantly reduce the metabolic cost. Drafting also has a psychological effect; it's much easier for runners to tuck in behind someone and let that runner pull them along than it is to maintain the pace on their own, so runners should let other runners do the work for as long as possible.

#66: Keep changing the pace.

While the best way to run the fastest possible time in a race is to run as even splits as possible, sometimes whom runners beat and the place in which they finish matters more than the time on the clock. In those races, a great winning racing strategy is to keep changing the pace on an opponent, in effect turning the race into a very hard fartlek. This strategy is very debilitating to other runners. If a runner can handle changing the pace throughout the race, this is a very big weapon to have in his arsenal. Since this strategy is so demanding, it must be practiced in workouts.

#67: Count steps.

While I usually advise runners to focus on what they're doing during a race and stay in the moment, sometimes runners just need to get their mind off the task at hand. Counting steps is a great way to do that. It helps to dissociate from the effort and focus on something other than the discomfort. Runners can count every time their right foot hits the ground for 100 steps. For the next 100 steps, they can try increasing the cadence slightly. Other tricks can be done to distract a runner's mind, including spelling words, singing a song in his head, calculating his pace, and counting the number of runners passed.

#68: Pass other runners with authority.

Every time athletes pass another runner in a race, they should pick up the pace as they go by. Athletes don't want to give someone false confidence that he can stay with them, which runners often try to do when someone comes up alongside them. If athletes slowly pass other runners like a wimp who lacks confidence, those runners will cling to them like refrigerator magnets. If athletes go past other runners with authority, they'll deflate those competitors, both physically and psychologically. The competitors will think the athletes look so strong while they're hurting. It will also make athletes feel strong and powerful since it always feels good to pass someone in a race, especially when doing so with authority. That momentum can carry athletes all the way to the finish line.

#69: Be strategic from behind.

One strategy often forgotten in the emotional context of racing is to race as strategically as possible. Runners should watch the competition from behind. As the great marathoner Bill Rodgers told me, the runner behind is often in control of the race, not the leader. Runners should only try for the lead or gain the edge on the competition when sensing the time is right, which may be when the lead pack has been reduced and they have fewer competitors to deal with. Runners should keep stalking opponents from behind and bide their time. If feeling great and sensing the competition is a bit off, runners may surge ahead and carry that momentum to the finish line.

#70: Be aware of the other runners.

When I was in high school, I ran a cross-country race in which I was leading the race, with a pack of runners from another school right off my shoulder. I was feeling very confident, like I was dictating the pace. With about half a mile to go, once we turned onto a different section of the course, the entire pack of runners went by me as if I were standing still. By the time I had realized what had happened, it was too late for me to respond to their move. They were too far ahead of me for me to catch them before the finish line. After the race, the coach of the other team came over to me and told me that was their plan all along; they knew I was the best runner on the other team, and they had singled me out before the race as they watched me warm up. They had planned for me to set the pace and do the work for most of the race and then make their move at a predetermined point, going by me all at once—and I fell for it. I was disappointed that I didn't win the race after leading it for so long, but I was even more disappointed that I let myself be duped. Their strategy worked because I didn't see it coming. If there's one race in my career that I wish I could run over again, that race is it.

All kinds of subtle things go on in a race, and it takes practice and experience to notice those things. When racing, runners should try to be aware of what's going on around them rather than letting the race pass them by. Runners should be aware of the other runners, how they may be working together, and be ready to react to their moves.

#71: Never look back.

Famous baseball pitcher Leroy "Satchel" Paige once said, "Don't look back. Something might be gaining on you." Nervous runners have a bad racing habit: they look over their shoulders. It's tempting to look back. Everyone has insecurities. Runners want to know where other runners are. Looking back over their shoulder during a race does nothing for race performance and gives the impression that runners are insecure and worried about the other runners. This approach gives opponents confidence runners don't want them to have. It's okay to be insecure; runners are human after all. They should just not let other runners know they're insecure. Runners must always focus on the race in front of them and what they have to do to keep moving forward.

#72: Breathe rhythmically.

In describing his run at the 1981 U.S. National 100-Kilometer Championships, ultramarathoner and zoologist Bernd Heinrich writes:

> The rhythm of my footsteps is steady, unvarying… it is unconsciously timed with my breathing… the breathing rhythm is usually also unconscious. It is timed to the same unconscious metronome that times the footsteps… Three steps with one long inspiration, a fourth step and a quick expiration. Over and over and over again. My mantra. (*Why We Run*, p. 248)

Many animals coordinate their breathing patterns to their stride rates. Animals that run on four legs seem to be constrained to a 1:1 ratio between steps and breaths, especially as speed increases. For example, the often-studied thoroughbred horse, which has remarkable aerobic capabilities, links breathing frequency 1:1 with stride rate, with inspiration and expiration always occurring at the same point in the stride. On the other end of the spectrum is the sluggish terrestrial turtle, which seems to be the only animal studied that does not link the two rhythms.

Unlike quadruped animals, humans use several step:breath ratios while running, including 2:1, 3:1, 4:1, 3:2, and 5:2, with a 2:1 ratio being the most common pattern. In runners who exhibit even step:breath ratios (e.g., 4:1 or 2:1), the beginning and end of the breathing cycle are associated with the same footfall. Coordinating the breathing rhythm to the stride rhythm is linked to running experience, with more fit and experienced runners exhibiting more coordination, often with a 2:1 step:breath ratio when running at faster speeds. With many miles of training, runners seem to subconsciously learn how to most effectively ventilate their lungs and minimize the metabolic cost of breathing, which may improve running economy. However, the two rhythms can be linked consciously, too. During training, runners should practice coordinating breathing to stride rate, taking three or four steps per breath during slower running speeds and two steps per breath at faster running speeds, always exhaling as the foot lands on the ground. Not only can coordinating these two rhythms help make a runner more economical, doing so can also provide something to focus on during a race.

#73: Divide.

Runners should think of a race in segments. There's nothing runners can do about the third lap of a mile race when running the first lap, and there's nothing runners can do about mile 24 of a marathon when running mile three. Runners should divide the race into smaller, more manageable segments and focus on each segment at a time. If aiming for a specific time goal, runners should focus on attaining that goal at each mile checkpoint. For example, if a runner wants to run a 5K in 16:00, he should focus on running each mile in 5:09. If a runner wants to run a three-hour marathon, he should focus on running each mile in 6:52. Runners should remember to not let their head get ahead of them. They should focus on getting to a certain checkpoint and not think beyond that checkpoint until they have reached it.

#74: Don't slow down.

I once heard a coach yell to her athletes during a race, "Don't slow down." While this may sound like good advice, telling a runner to not slow down isn't going to prevent the runner from slowing down. That's like telling someone, "Don't think about a pink elephant." When told not to do something, that statement reinforces the undesirable behavior or habit rather than reinforcing the desirable behavior or habit. Furthermore, without the skills in place, the verbal command "Don't slow down" has little effect. That's like telling a depressed person, "Don't be depressed." It doesn't work. The runner must learn, through repeated practice, how not to slow down or, rather, how to maintain or pick up the pace. Most people don't respond well to negative feedback or negative reinforcement. People respond better to positive feedback and positive reinforcement. So if any spectators or coaches are watching a race, they should say positive things to runners rather than "Don't slow down." When racing, runners want to be thinking about what to do, not about what not to do. Understanding the many variables that go into smart training and running a winning race and then executing a winning race plan will not only prevent runners from slowing down, it will enable them to run faster in the latter stages of the race when everyone else is slowing down.

#75: Use the other runners in the race to bring out the competitive animal inside.

While some people are naturally more competitive than others, all people have a competitive instinct, as it is necessary for evolution and natural selection. Without competition, no advantage exists that could favor organisms to carry a new and advantageous mutation over older organisms not carrying such an advantage. Thus, without competition there wouldn't be natural selection or an upward trend in evolution. The primary pressure driving human sociality is competition from other human groups. By competing within his own species, humankind supports the chances for success of its biological information in future generations. Thus, it is likely that humans competed primarily with others of their own species for reproductive success. Humans do not perform behaviors that are for the good of their species. Natural selection favors selfish behavior because altruistic acts only serve to increase the recipient's reproductive success while decreasing that of the donor's. It's survival of the fittest in its most literal form.

Runners should not be timid about competing against the other runners in a race. They can be friends before the race starts and after it is over, but during the race, there is no such thing as friendship, only animals in the heat of battle. While an individual will always be his biggest competitor, other runners, when in the heat of battle, can bring out things inside of him that he never thought possible.

#76: Draw on deeper emotions.

Emotions can be very powerful. Drawing on deeper emotions during a race stimulates the secretion of hormones, which can help improve performance. Both physical and psychological stress are associated with an increased secretion of stress hormones, notably epinephrine (adrenaline), norepinephrine (noradrenaline), and cortisol. The increase in cortisol secretion, which is positively associated with the intensity and duration of exercise, stimulates protein catabolism in muscle to provide the liver with amino acids for gluconeogenesis (the formation of new glucose from non-carbohydrate sources) and thus provides more fuel during competition. Competitive and psychologically stressful situations augment the cortisol response to exercise, further increasing the availability of fuel. Given the depletion of muscle glycogen and the hypoglycemia (low blood glucose) characteristic of the marathon, cortisol's stimulation of gluconeogenesis may exert its greatest effects on performance in the marathon.

Hormones aside, there's also an inexplicable side to the powerful effect of emotions. They can bring people to places they never thought possible. My father died when I was eight years old. My mother died a few months before the writing of this book. Sometimes, when I am running a race, I draw on the deep emotions I have about losing my parents. In those moments, I am in a place where no one knows, where no one can be but me. It is a place made up of anger, fear, emotional distress, and love. It is a cathartic experience. I draw on those emotions to fulfill my physical potential. It is so draining that I can do it only on certain occasions. I'm pretty sure there's no scientific explanation for this. If this could be explained by scientists, people would never have the opportunity to be amazed by their achievements or be swept away by their own emotions. So runners should draw on deeper emotions and be amazed at the outcome.

4

Other Winning Racing Strategies

#77: Learn from past races.

Whether runners have a good or bad race, they can learn things from each race that will enable them to run a better race in the future. When runners have a good race, they should try to figure out what went right and why. Did they run even splits? Were they focused on racing the other runners rather than on the stopwatch? Were they rested going into the race? Did they do a good job of not giving up? Did they respond well to other runners' moves? Did they attack the hills? For their next race, runners should duplicate whatever it was that worked. When they have a bad race, runners should try to figure out what went wrong and why. Were they fatigued going into the race? Was the training leading up to the race too hard? Did they start off too fast? Were they unable to respond to other runners' moves? Did any outside pressures or stresses contribute to the outcome? If runners can isolate why they had a bad race, they can help to avoid another bad race for the same reason in the future. Runners should write down the good things and bad things from each race.

Each race is an opportunity to learn. Things like correct pacing strategy, other runners' strengths and weaknesses, runners' own strengths and weaknesses, how they handle pressure, even how much they're willing to be physically uncomfortable are all things that can be learned with each race. Runners should take advantage of the opportunity and learn as much as they can.

#78: Know the *why* behind the *how*.

When I was a runner in high school, I was told by an Olympic 400-meter runner that runners who know why they are doing what they are doing will beat runners who only know how to do it. Many runners know how to run fast because they have genes given to them from their parents, which allow them to run fast. When runners understand why they should train and race a certain way, they become invested in the process. They can beat other runners in races because they understand why a specific strategy leads to a specific result. That's a higher level of understanding than simply knowing how. Knowledge is knowing that water is composed of two atoms of hydrogen and one atom of oxygen—H_2O. Understanding why those atoms of hydrogen and oxygen interact the way they do allows a person to understand the nature of water so well that he can make it rain.

#79: Understand estrogen and what it can do for female runners.

Whether they are milers or ultramarathoners, estrogen is the single biggest thing that differentiates female runners from the guys running next to them in a race. It is a powerful hormone, influencing many aspects of a woman's physiology, from glycogen storage to lung function to bone health. The more that is learned about estrogen, the more runner-friendly it seems.

A woman's hormonal environment is constantly changing as a result of the menstrual cycle, the defining physiological characteristic of females, which occurs monthly from menarche (ages 11 to 14) until menopause (ages 45 to 55). Any physiological changes resulting from menstrual cycle-induced fluctuations in estrogen (and progesterone) are exacerbated when running, especially if it's intense, as it is in most races. When a woman goes for a hard run or races, the concentrations of estrogen and progesterone in the blood increase during both the follicular (days 1 to 14) and luteal (days 15 to 28) phases of the menstrual cycle.

Racing across the menstrual cycle is a complicated matter. Although a number of studies have found endurance exercise performance to vary between phases of the menstrual cycle, an equal number of studies report no differences in endurance performance. Menstrual phase variations in endurance performance may largely be a consequence of changes to exercise metabolism that are stimulated by the fluctuations in the concentrations of estrogen and progesterone. Anecdotally, many women claim that they don't run well in the few days surrounding their periods.

If endurance performance is better at certain times of the month, it seems that, in general, it is better during the middle part of the luteal phase of the menstrual cycle (days 20 to 24), which is characterized by high progesterone and rising estrogen. However, endurance performance may only be improved in the mid-luteal phase compared with the follicular phase when the ratio of estrogen to progesterone is high (i.e., the increase in estrogen concentration is high relative to the increase in progesterone concentration). Performance may also be better during the late follicular phase (days 8 to 14), which is characterized by the pre-ovulatory surge in estrogen and suppressed progesterone concentrations.

Estrogen promotes a greater use of fat for energy as the limited store of carbohydrate (glycogen) is spared and stimulates a greater storage of muscle glycogen, both of which are important characteristics for long races. When planning to run a marathon or ultramarathon, races that are greatly influenced by the amount of glycogen stored in skeletal muscles, female runners should try to plan it to coincide with the mid-luteal phase of the menstrual cycle. Research has shown that women with a normal or high carbohydrate diet have a greater muscle glycogen content during the mid-luteal phase of the menstrual cycle compared to the mid-follicular phase; however, the amount of muscle glycogen in the mid-follicular phase can be made greater with a high carbohydrate diet.

While the high concentration of estrogen during the luteal phase can improve long-endurance performance due to its effects on metabolism and glycogen storage, the high concentration of progesterone during the luteal phase increases body temperature and negatively affects fluid balance, causing a loss of water and electrolytes. This can be bad news for long races like the marathon, since both hyperthermia and dehydration, through their effects on stroke volume and cardiac output, cause fatigue in the marathon. Therefore, if the date of the marathon falls during her luteal phase, when progesterone is high, a female runner should do whatever she can to keep her body temperature from rising and stay as hydrated as possible.

#80: Always remain positive.

One of the distinguishing characteristics of successful athletes is their unrelenting ability to remain positive, even in the face of negative circumstances. People often cannot control what happens to them, but they can control how they respond to what happens to them. Remaining positive when details before or after a race don't go as planned will go a long way to keeping runners calm and helping them to run a great race. It's easy for negative thoughts to enter a runner's head when things aren't going according to plan during a race. It's important for runners to notice those thoughts and immediately refocus their thinking on the process. Part of having a positive mental attitude is being able to move past bad workouts or races. If a runner goes into a race thinking he's not going to do well, he likely won't. Even if a runner's training hasn't gone as well as he wanted, he's not feeling well, he just broke up with a significant other, or whatever the negative case may be, when stepping to the starting line, a runner must remove all negative thoughts and replace them with positive ones. Runners owe that to themselves. At the starting line, none of those negative things matter. The only thing that matters is the race in front of them.

#81: Prevent injuries.

While sometimes runners get injured without any apparent reason and no matter how careful they are, a number of factors can predict the likelihood of a runner getting injured. The problem is that runners and coaches don't often take the time or make the effort to identify them. Many injuries can be prevented if runners are screened for the following risk factors.

Low Energy Availability

Given the large number of calories expended from many miles of running, runners need to make sure they consume enough calories to offset their high caloric expenditure. Many runners simply don't eat enough to meet their needs for specific nutrients, like calcium and Vitamin D, which can put bones at risk for injury. Low energy availability is a key risk factor for stress fractures, especially among female runners. Runners need to consume 1,000 milligrams of calcium per day and 400 International Units of Vitamin D per day.

Female Athlete Triad

The largest risk for stress fractures in female runners occurs when they have one or more of three associated characteristics—menstrual irregularities, disordered eating, and osteoporosis—collectively called the female athlete triad. High training volumes can cause irregular or even absent menstrual cycles (amenorrhea), which increase the risk for osteoporosis and stress fractures. Research has shown that female athletes with irregular menstruation or amenorrhea have a lower bone mineral density than female athletes with normal menstruation. Disordered eating (not to be confused with an eating disorder, like anorexia or bulimia), common among female runners due to external or self-imposed pressure to lose weight, may result in caloric restriction, and is independently associated with both irregular menstruation and low bone mineral density. In other words, a runner could have normal menstruation and still have low bone mineral density if her dietary habits are inadequate to meet her caloric needs. If runners have any of the characteristics of the female athlete triad, they should regularly have their bone mineral density assessed to determine if they are at risk for injury. If they do have low bone mineral density, they may want to take birth control pills, which provide bone-protecting estrogen.

Previous Injury

Runners who have had an injury are at an increased risk for another one. Already having an injury shows that body part is vulnerable.

Large Increases in Training Load

The majority of injuries—including tendonitis and stress fractures—result from doing too much too soon. For example, the common injury of shin splints (medial tibial stress syndrome), which occurs most often in newer and younger runners, is typically caused by exposure to excessive shock to which the bone is initially unable to adapt. To prevent large increases in training load, runners should increase the length and intensity of their runs by no more than 10 to 15 percent per week and back off on the volume for one week every few weeks to allow the body to adapt to the training, recover from the training stress, and stay injury-free. Following are some training guidelines for preventing running-related injuries:

- *Increase mileage by no more than one mile per day per week.* If currently running 20 miles in four days per week, athletes should run no more than 24 miles next week by adding one mile to each of the four days. They should not run 24 miles the next week by adding all four miles to only one day of running. Highly-trained runners can get away with adding more miles more quickly, especially if they have experience running more miles.
- *Run the same mileage for three to four weeks before increasing it.* Runners need to give the legs a chance to adapt to each level of running before increasing the level.
- *Back off training by about a third for one recovery week before increasing the training load.* If a runner has been running 30 miles per week for three weeks, he should back off to 20 miles for one week before increasing above 30 miles for next week.
- *Never increase volume and intensity at the same time.* When beginning to include speedwork, runners should either drop overall mileage for the week or maintain mileage from where it was prior to adding speedwork. They should never add more miles to the week at same time as introducing speedwork.
- *Get adequate recovery.* All adaptations from training occur during recovery from training, not during the training itself. The older runners are, the more time they need to recover from training, so the longer they need before increasing volume and intensity. Young runners can get away with training mistakes; older runners cannot.

Strength Imbalances

Muscle strength imbalances, like those between the quadriceps and the hamstrings and between the calves and the muscles on the front of the shin can lead to muscle and tendon injuries. Runners should attend to these imbalances by strengthening their weaker muscles.

Lack of Running Experience

Runners who lack experience are at a great risk for injuries. Therefore, extra care must be taken when increasing the volume and intensity of inexperienced runners' training. Inexperienced runners may need to spend a few weeks at the same training load before increasing the load.

Inappropriate Running Shoes

The best running shoe is the shoe that is right for the individual runner's foot type and running mechanics. Running shoes have specific combinations of support and stability designed for different running gaits. Cushioning shoes, which are best suited for runners with normal to high arches, promote adequate pronation to absorb shock upon landing. Stability shoes, which are best suited for runners with normal to low arches and who slightly overpronate, allow only limited pronation and retain some cushioning characteristics. Motion control shoes, which are best suited for runners with flat feet and who severely overpronate, prevent pronation. Running in the wrong shoes can adversely affect lower extremity alignment, making runners more susceptible to injury. For example, predisposing factors for Achilles tendonitis include a shoe that twists easily, insufficient heel height, and a rigid sole. Running shoes should be replaced after 300 to 400 miles because they lose their shock-absorbing abilities.

#82: Write down goals.

Goals are important for many reasons, not the least of which is that they provide runners with direction. It's important to write goals on paper so they are tangible. Runners should write them down every day. The goals should be specific, realistic, and set to a specific timeline. The piece of paper should be placed where it will be seen multiple times per day, like the bathroom mirror or the back of the front door.

#83: Focus on the process rather than the outcome.

Runners are often focused on what time they want to see on the stopwatch or clock when the race is over. After all, runners get caught up in numbers. It's hard not to; runners like to see results. However, outcomes, like what time runners want to run, are often not controllable. What matters is the process, since that is within an individual's control. Runners should focus on each mile they are running when they are running it and what they are doing each step of the race. They should focus on passing other runners, focus on breathing and trying to remain relaxed, and focus on stride and how powerful they feel. By focusing on these process-oriented factors, the outcome will often take care of itself.

#84: Ask friends and family to watch the race.

No one wants to do things in anonymity. People may have moments when they want to be alone, when their more private side comes out, but, ultimately, humans are social animals. They want to share. When people accomplish things, they want to share those accomplishments with other people in their lives. They want others to watch them do what they do. Having friends and family in attendance at races is a winning racing strategy because it will help athletes run faster than they normally would. Everyone wants to show off, even if only a little. This phenomenon is also backed by research, which has shown that people can do more physical work when they are encouraged by others. For example, in a laboratory during a $\dot{V}O_2$max test, the atmosphere is exciting, with a number of people cheering and encouraging the person running on the treadmill, just like at a race. When runners have people they know cheering for them at a race, the race becomes something more than just all about them; with friends and family present, runners are doing it for those in attendance, too, and that helps improve performance.

#85: Wear the right shoes.

People don't go to a business meeting in sandals, do they? How about a cocktail party in sneakers? The right shoes are worn for the right occasion. When racing on the track, runners wear spikes. When racing on the road, they wear road-racing shoes. When racing on trails, runners wear trail shoes, which have more traction on the sole compared to road-running shoes. When racing, shoes should feel very comfortable, as if they are an extension of the feet. Runners should take the time to get the right shoes.

#86: Be a hero.

Every race has a moment when it starts to feel uncomfortable. While it's a natural human tendency to back off from physical discomfort for self-preservation, one of the things that makes runners unique is their penchant for seeking it out. It is in that moment in the race that runners learn about themselves and what they are willing to do to meet their goal. Do they back off from the pain, or do they address the pain and push through it? Racing gives runners a chance to discover the answer and, in so exploring, become who they want to be. Runners want to walk away from a race feeling like they gave it everything they had. They want to be proud of themselves. Racing provides runners the opportunity to become better than they currently are—to become their own hero.

#87: Get educated.

To run winning races, athletes need to understand what is involved in becoming a more accomplished runner. They should take the time to learn about the sport by reading the works of notable coaches and runners, reading books on running, understanding how to train most effectively, and understanding the purpose of training. When working with a coach, runners should ask him to explain the reasons for the training methods. Knowledge is power. Runners shouldn't believe everything they hear from other runners or coaches. The more knowledge and understanding runners have about what they're doing, the more they become a part of the process and the more likely they are to be successful.

#88: Become tough.

One of my former athletes, commenting on why many of the best college distance running teams in the country are in cold climates, used to say that running in cold, icy, snowy weather makes runners tougher. There may be something to that. Distance running is a demanding sport. It's not a sport for high-maintenance or soft people. Runners have to be willing to be physically uncomfortable, and they have to know how to handle that discomfort. If runners have an inner strength, racing is the time to use it because racing brings that inner strength to the surface. Running is often used as a metaphor for life because, just as people have moments in life that are difficult and test their resolve, runners have moments in races and in training that are difficult and test their resolve. It's a very clear parallel. When the effort becomes uncomfortable, do runners back off the pace, or do they push through that discomfort for the self-discovery that lies on the other side? Successful runners have a certain toughness about them, a willingness to be uncomfortable, a willingness to train despite less than ideal climatic conditions. While having that toughness, like a high $\dot{V}O_2$max, is largely genetic, runners can acquire toughness through training, as they become more capable of tolerating high degrees of physical discomfort. While running easy every day is easy, runners shouldn't shy away from difficult workouts, as those workouts will help them develop the toughness they need to run winning races.

#89: Be patient.

People want things right away. But, like many worthwhile things in life, both racing and training require patience to be successful. In a race, runners need to hold back the pace even when others have taken the pace out too fast. While it may feel easy, especially in a long race like the marathon, to run the first mile of the race at the same pace as the last, patience will pay huge dividends during that last mile. Same is true for races on the track. It's easy to take the pace out fast the first couple of laps, but being patient will allow runners to finish faster than other runners. In training, runners need to be patient while they log the miles to develop themselves aerobically. It's easy to just run fast workouts to see success sooner. But being patient and doing the necessary aerobic work first, which takes a significant amount of time, will make athletes better overall runners and will raise their level of performance. The short-term, quick-fix approach rarely works for a distance runner, so stock up on patience.

#90: Eat a high carbohydrate diet.

The many proponents of diets like Atkins and South Beach would have the public believe that carbohydrates are some kind of poison. However, carbohydrates are a runner's best friend. Carbohydrates are free as sugar (glucose) in the blood and stored in skeletal muscles and the liver as glycogen (a branched chain of glucose molecules). When running, athletes use a combination of blood glucose and glycogen as fuel to regenerate energy for muscle contraction. Carbohydrates are the muscles' preferred fuel during exercise. The ability to perform endurance exercise is strongly influenced by the amount of pre-exercise glycogen stored in skeletal muscles, with muscle glycogen depletion becoming the decisive factor limiting prolonged exercise. When running, athletes lower their carbohydrate fuel tank. Consuming carbohydrates immediately afterward quickly refills the fuel tank so they have adequate fuel for the next workout. The rapidity with which runners recover from a long or intense workout will dictate how often they can perform other long or intense workouts, which may ultimately influence the ability to reach their running potential. Athletes can't effectively train like a distance runner if they have a diet low in carbohydrates. That will only make them feel sluggish and flat. When training hard, runners should consume at least 60 percent of their calories from carbohydrates.

Many people think that carbohydrates are bad and lead to weight gain. But that only happens when they don't exercise. It is a metabolic priority of recovering muscle to replenish glycogen stores because carbohydrate is the preferred fuel for muscles. If a person doesn't run, there is never a drain on muscle glycogen, so any carbohydrates consumed that are not used to meet the metabolic needs of the muscles are stored as fat. Conversely, if a person continually creates a metabolic demand by running every day and lowering the carbohydrate fuel tank, the carbohydrates consumed will go to replace what was used during training and not get stored as fat.

#91: Drink chocolate milk immediately after workouts and races.

To recover quickly from training and racing, runners must refuel nutrient-depleted muscles. The two most important nutrients to replenish are carbohydrates and protein. Research has shown that chocolate milk is an ideal post-run recovery drink because it is high in both carbohydrates and protein.

Endurance performance is strongly influenced by the amount of stored carbohydrate in muscles (glycogen), with intense endurance exercise decreasing muscle glycogen content. Thus, recovery is closely linked to the replenishment of carbohydrates. Muscles are picky when it comes to the time for synthesizing and storing glycogen. Although glycogen will continue to be synthesized until storage in the muscles is complete, the process is most rapid if carbohydrates are consumed within the first 30 to 60 minutes after a workout or race. Indeed, delaying carbohydrate ingestion for two hours after a workout significantly reduces the rate of glycogen resynthesis. To maximize the synthesis and storage of glycogen, runners should consume 0.7 gram of simple carbohydrate (sugar, preferably glucose) per pound of body weight immediately after a workout and every two hours for a few hours afterward.

Protein is also important for optimal recovery since protein is used to repair skeletal muscle fibers that have been damaged during training. Runners should consume 20 to 30 grams of complete protein within 30 to 60 minutes after a workout. Complete proteins—like meat, poultry, fish, eggs, milk, cheese, yogurt, and soy products—contain all the essential amino acids to help rebuild muscle. Since nutrients from fluids are absorbed more quickly than from solid foods, carbohydrates and protein should initially be consumed from fluids.

#92: Increase stride length.

Running speed equals stride length times stride rate. If runners want to get faster, they have to increase either or both of these stride components. Coaches often tell their athletes to do specific workouts to increase their stride rates. However, stride length increases preferentially over stride rate with increasing distance running speed. Stride rate changes only slightly, hovering between 80 to 90 steps per minute with each leg. The stability in stride rate also occurs as speed decreases due to fatigue. Faster runners don't necessarily take more steps than slower runners. Stride length explains a much greater amount of variance in speed compared to stride rate. The subconscious manipulation of stride length and stride rate at different speeds may be governed by what is most economical for the runner, such that there is a most economical stride length at a given speed and a most economical stride rate at all distance running speeds. So, if runners want to get faster, they need to focus on increasing stride length by increasing hip extension at push-off (not by reaching the leg out in front of them) and by increasing the amount of force produced against the ground at push-off rather than trying to take quicker steps.

#93: Own the process.

Racing isn't something that just happens. To run a winning race, one that runners can be proud of, they must take ownership of the process. They should not just let things and other runners pass them by. Runners need to know when to hold back and when to take control of certain moments in the race. They should avoid going into the race thinking, "I'm just going to run and see what happens." Rather, they should go into the race thinking, "This is what I want to accomplish, so this is what I'm going to do." Runners should become an integral part of the racing process and take responsibility for their thoughts and actions before, during, and after the race.

#94: Develop a personal definition of "winning."

While this book is called *101 Winning Racing Strategies for Runners*, winning doesn't always mean coming in first place. After all, only one runner in the race comes in first place; everyone else finishes in something other than first place. Running a winning race does not and should not always mean finishing first. To place the emphasis on winning would make a lot of people disappointed. Running a winning race may mean finishing first if a runner has the talent and circumstances to do so. But it also can mean running a personal record, beating a specific opponent, executing a race plan, running a strong, strategic race, or doing the best he can do on that day. Runners have to define what "winning" means to them. What result will make them satisfied? How do they measure success? Going into a race, the most important thing is that runners finish the race feeling like they could not have done any better on that day. Regardless of the outcome—the time on the clock and the place they have finished—what matters most is that runners walk away from the race feeling that they gave it everything they had and that they can honestly say that they could not have done any better on that day. That alone is something to be immensely proud of and is worth the price of admission.

#95: Don't race when fatigued.

Heavy training, while necessary for high-level performance, is accompanied by fatigue. Runners should not attempt to run a race during periods of heavy training; otherwise, they may be disappointed in the result. To run a winning race, runners need to be rested and fresh. It's hard to race well during periods of hard training, which are accompanied by microscopic muscle fiber damage and elevated levels of stress hormones. This need for rest becomes a problem for high school runners, who are expected to race many times during the school year, often twice per week. Overracing has its own set of problems, not the least of which is the sacrifice of aerobic development and the potential for physical and mental burnout. Thus, high school runners have to train through many early season races, leaving them too fatigued to race well. The best time to run a race is after a period of recovery. When racing in the middle of hard training, runners should understand that the race is part of the training rather than the goal being trained for.

#96: Don't race without the proper conditioning.

I often get emails from people asking me what training they should do for their upcoming marathon that is three months away. My first response is that they shouldn't run a marathon on only three months of training, unless they have already been running for many months. Races have become so popular, the marathon in particular, that many people want to run them just to say that they've done it. The preparation that's needed is often pushed to the side, dismissed as an afterthought. Hundreds of thousands of people in the U.S. run marathons on no more than 30 to 35 miles of running per week. How anyone can be confident going to the starting line of a 26.2-mile race having run only 30 to 35 miles per week is difficult to imagine. Many runners run races without the proper conditioning. Whether running a marathon or a mile, racing before being properly conditioned will only lead to disappointment. It can also invite injury because the body is not properly prepared for the stress of racing. Before attempting to race, runners need to spend time conditioning themselves. If runners take the time and do the training, they will run a much better race.

#97: Know strengths and weaknesses, and race to the strengths.

Everyone has different talents. To run a winning race, runners must first know themselves. What are their strengths and weaknesses as a runner and racer? Are they able to hang with competitors during the middle stages, but get outkicked in the last quarter to half mile? Do they have a hard time maintaining the pace during the middle stages, but can finish fast and outkick others? Do they have a good sense of pace? Are they impatient? Do they get overly nervous? How good is their finishing kick and how far from the finish line can they sustain it? Runners should learn their strengths and weaknesses and how they can use them to their advantage. For example, if a runner is a great kicker, then he needs to plan to stay close enough to an opponent to outkick him in the final stages of the race. If a runner knows he is not a good kicker, then he needs to put some distance between himself and his competitor before the latter stages of the race so he doesn't get outkicked. If a runner knows he is impatient, then he needs to make a move early so he doesn't get too anxious late in the race. Some runners are more comfortable leading the race, and some are more comfortable following.

#98: Commit to being challenged.

One of the great things about racing is that it gives runners the opportunity to challenge themselves. There aren't too many other situations or environments in life in which a person knows going in that he'll have such a clear opportunity. Runners should take advantage of that opportunity. Before the race, runners should commit to challenging themselves and use the race as a way to find out who they really are.

#99: Don't do anything new on race day.

The day of the race is not the time to do anything different. Runners should wear the same shoes they have been wearing in training. They should not buy new shoes to wear in the race. When racing on a track or cross-country course and wearing spikes for the race, runners should make sure to have done a few workouts in the spikes. The longer the race, the more important it is to not do anything new. For the marathon, runners should wear the same clothes in addition to the same shoes they've been wearing in training. Shorts, socks, what they plan to carry on them (such as water, GU packs, etc.), nothing should be new. Everything—clothes, pre-race meal, warm-up—should be tested in training first.

#100: Don't give away secrets.

Running is such an old sport and there are so many runners and running coaches that everyone involved in the sport thinks they already know everything. Are there really any secrets to running winning races? Of course there are. This book is filled with them. By applying the secrets in this book, athletes can run better races and have a huge advantage over their opponents—as long as they don't tell anyone else the secrets!

#101: Learn the right moves.

I have a friend who has a son who was born without a right arm. His name is Billy. When Billy was born, his mother was very worried, because she knew how difficult life would be for Billy. But she promised herself that she would try to give Billy as normal of a life as possible. When Billy was seven years old, he asked his mother if he could take karate lessons. At first, his mother was nervous at the idea. After all, karate can be very dangerous, especially for someone missing an arm. But she remembered the promise she made to herself, so she agreed, hoping that Billy would be okay.

The first day of karate class, Billy met his sensei, who taught him a move and had him practice it. At the end of the first class, he sent Billy home and told him to come back next week. The next week, the sensei showed Billy the same move and had Billy practice it. Billy practiced the move again the following week, and the week after that, and the week after that.

After a couple of months of lessons, the sensei said to Billy, "Billy, I think you are ready for your first karate tournament."

Billy couldn't believe his ears. "What?" he said, startled at the idea. "How can I be ready to compete? I've only learned one move and I only have one arm."

"Don't worry. You're ready," said the sensei confidently.

Billy was so nervous that he didn't tell his friends at school; he didn't even tell his mother. He went alone with the sensei to the karate tournament. In his first match of the tournament, Billy nervously stood on the mat, facing his opponent. He didn't know what the heck to do. He had never been in this position before. He looked over to the sensei, shrugged his shoulders, and asked, "What do I do?"

The sensei looked right at him and replied, "Do the move."

So, Billy did the move, and he won the match. For his second match, again he was nervous. He stood on the mat, facing his opponent. Again, he looked over to the sensei, shrugged his shoulders, and asked, "What do I do?"

The sensei replied, "Do the move."

So, Billy did the move, and he won the match. For his third match, again he was nervous, albeit a bit more confident than he was before. He stood on the mat, facing his opponent. Again, unsure of what to do against his stronger, more experienced opponent, he looked over to the sensei and asked, "What do I do?"

The sensei replied, "Do the move."

So, Billy did the move, and he won the match. Billy did the move, the only one he knew, a few more times, winning each of his matches, until he made it to the finals.

With each round of the tournament, he gained confidence. For the final championship match against the defending champion, Billy stood on the mat, facing his opponent. This time, he looked over to the sensei, but no words needed to be spoken. Billy nodded his head. The sensei nodded his head. Billy did the move, and he won the championship match. The crowd was on its feet. Billy was ecstatic. He had never accomplished anything like this before.

During the ride home, Billy said to the sensei, "I don't understand. How was I able to win the karate tournament? I only know one move, and I don't have…"

The sensei stopped him before he could finish the sentence. "Billy," he said authoritatively, "You have mastered the most difficult move in karate. There is only one defense for that move. For your opponent to defend that move, he would have to grab your right arm."

Like Billy winning the karate tournament, running a winning race is about learning the right moves. Using the 101 strategies in this book, runners can make their next race a winning one.

About the Author

Jason Karp, Ph.D., is a nationally recognized running coach, freelance writer and author, and exercise physiologist. He owns RunCoachJason.com, a state-of-the-science running coaching and personal training company in San Diego, California. As a running expert and the 2011 IDEA Personal Trainer of the Year, Karp is a trusted source of information. Through his writing, conference presentations, DVDs, and numerous print and television interviews on topics related to running and fitness, he brings the state of the science directly to the public. A sought-after speaker, he is a frequent presenter at national fitness, coaching, and academic conferences and has been profiled in a number of publications. He has taught USA Track & Field's highest level coaching certification and was an instructor at the USATF/U.S. Olympic Committee's Emerging Elite Coaches Camp at the U.S. Olympic Training Center. He also regularly holds clinics for runners, coaches, and fitness professionals. He is a prolific writer, with over 200 articles published in numerous international coaching, running, and fitness trade and consumer magazines, including *Track Coach, Techniques for Track & Field and Cross Country, New Studies in Athletics, Athletics Weekly, Running Times, Runner's World, Trail Runner, Women's Running, Marathon & Beyond, IDEA Fitness Journal, Shape,* and *Ultra-Fit,* among others. He is also author of three other books, including *How to Survive Your PhD* (Sourcebooks, 2009), *101 Developmental Concepts & Workouts for Cross Country Runners* (Coaches Choice, 2010), and *Running for Women* (Human Kinetics, 2012).

In 1997, at the age of 24, Karp became one of the youngest head college coaches in the country, leading the Georgian Court University (NJ) women's cross country team to the regional championship, and was named NAIA Northeast Region Coach of the Year. He has coached cross country and track at the high school, college, and elite club levels. His personal training experience ranges from elite athletes to cardiac rehab patients. As a private coach and founder of *REVO$_2$LT Running Team*™, he has helped many runners meet their potential, ranging from a first-time race participant to an Olympic Trials qualifier. A competitive runner, Karp is a nationally certified running coach through USA Track & Field and is sponsored by PowerBar® as a member of PowerBar Team Elite™.

Karp received his Ph.D. in exercise physiology with a physiology minor from Indiana University in 2007, his master's degree in kinesiology from the University of Calgary in 1997, and his bachelor's degree in exercise and sport science with an English minor from Pennsylvania State University in 1995. His research has included motor unit recruitment during eccentric muscle contractions, post-exercise nutrition for optimal recovery in endurance athletes, training characteristics of Olympic marathon trials qualifiers, and the coordination of breathing and stride rate in distance runners. His research has been published in the scientific journals *Medicine and Science in Sports and Exercise*, *International Journal of Sport Nutrition and Exercise Metabolism*, and *International Journal of Sports Physiology and Performance*. Karp has taught at several universities and currently teaches applied exercise physiology at Miramar College in San Diego and dissertation writing, a course he designed for doctoral students, at the University of California, San Diego.